Anton Anderson and Paul Latham

THE SCIENCE OF BUILDING ACCOUNTANT PARTNERSHIPS

How Financial Advisors Can Form Strategic Partnerships to Attract and Keep High-Net-Worth Clients

THE
Short Book Formula
PUBLISHING

Published by The Short Book Formula

DISCLAIMER

This book contains the opinions and ideas of the authors and is intended for educational and informational purposes only. Nothing contained in this publication constitutes financial, investment, tax, legal, or compliance advice. Every individual's financial situation is unique, and readers should consult with qualified professionals who can evaluate their specific circumstances, needs, and goals before making any financial decisions.

The strategies, frameworks, revenue projections, and examples discussed herein are illustrative in nature and do not represent guaranteed outcomes. All financial figures, close rates, fee structures, and revenue projections are hypothetical examples based on historical internal data and individual experiences, which may not be representative of typical results. Past performance is not indicative of future results. Individual outcomes will vary significantly based on compliance requirements, market conditions, personal effort, and other factors.

Readers are strongly encouraged to consult their broker-dealer compliance department, legal counsel, and qualified financial and tax advisors before implementing any strategy described in this book. No reader should act or refrain from acting based solely on the information contained in this book without first seeking appropriate professional advice

Any use of the information found in this book is the sole responsibility of the reader. The authors, publisher, Elite Resource Team, VFO Services, and any affiliated entities disclaim any liability for actions taken or not taken based on the contents of this book.

CONTENTS

FOREWORD BY

Ronald J. Baker

The accounting profession has a pricing problem. And as a financial advisor, that problem is your opportunity.

Having spent decades challenging the status quo of the accounting profession through my work at the VeraSage Institute and books like *The Firm of the Future and Pricing on Purpose*, I've seen firsthand how deeply rooted that problem is. For years, accountants have been selling time when they should have been selling transformation. They have been billing for inputs when clients only ever cared about outcomes. The result is a profession trapped in a model that commoditizes expertise, undervalues relationships, and leaves its best clients underserved. And I can tell you with confidence, the best accountants know it. They are actively looking for a way out.

I have long argued that the firm of the future does not look like the firm of the past. It does not bill by the hour or compete on price. It measures success by the value it creates for the people it serves.

That future is not theoretical. It is available right now to any professional willing to make the leap. What I did not fully anticipate was that, for many accountants, the catalyst for that leap would come from a financial advisor walking through their door with the right proposition.

This book shows you exactly how to be that advisor.

In *The Science of Building Accountant Partnerships*, Anton Anderson and Paul Latham lay out a systematic, field-tested method for financial advisors to build deep strategic partnerships with accountants, and in doing so, give those accountants access to a Virtual Family Office that fundamentally changes what they can offer their best clients. At its core, this is a book about helping accountants escape a broken model and positioning yourself as the partner who makes that possible.

Accounting firms do not have a knowledge problem. They have a business model problem. Most are still operating with outdated structures in a marketplace that has moved on, serving clients whose needs have far outgrown what a compliance-focused practice can deliver. When you understand that, you stop seeing accountants as referral sources and start seeing them as partners waiting to be unlocked. This book gives you a practical way to do exactly that.

The firm of the future will be built on relationships, not transactions. As a financial advisor, you have a rare opportunity to help shape that future for the accountants in your market and to build something meaningful in the process. This book is your blueprint.

— Ronald J. Baker

Founder, VeraSage Institute | Author of *The Firm of the Future and Pricing on Purpose*

FOREWORD BY

Dr. Jackie Meyer

In a world where the role of the financial advisor is rapidly evolving, *The Science of Building Accountant Partnerships* arrives at exactly the right moment. As a CPA, founder, and someone who has spent years helping accountants move beyond compliance into more proactive, advisory-focused roles, I've worked closely with firms navigating this shift. One thing is clear. The opportunity created by the right partnerships is significant, and it often goes untapped.

Gone are the days when advisors could afford to grow their practices through cold outreach, expensive marketing, and competing for the same pool of prospects as everyone else. Today's most successful advisors are not just managing wealth. They are building ecosystems, and the accountant sitting across town may be the most valuable relationship you haven't fully leveraged yet.

This isn't about adding more to your already full plate. It's about shifting your strategy. The advisors who will thrive in the years ahead are not necessarily the ones who work harder. They are the ones who build smarter through trusted, collaborative partnerships that generate warm introductions, deepen client relationships, and create more sustainable growth.

What Anton Anderson and Paul Latham have built here is more than a guide to forming accountant relationships. It is a complete, step-by-step system for identifying the right partners, approaching them with genuine value, and structuring a collaboration that benefits everyone involved, especially with the clients at the center of it all. Through practical frameworks, proven scripts, and real-world examples, this book removes the guesswork and provides a clear path forward.

If you have ever sensed that accountants could be a powerful source of growth for your practice but were not sure how to make it work in a meaningful and lasting way, this is your starting point. It is not just a guide for changing how you prospect. It is a foundation for changing how you grow.

— Dr. Jackie Meyer

PART 1

Who This Book Is For

Welcome! This book is aimed at **Financial Advisors** who currently offer (or aspire to) financial planning services to wealthy and financially-successful clients and who want to grow their business further by building Accountant Partnerships.

Most Financial Advisors are suffering from the impact of ***"commoditization"*** in their industry.

The typical Advisor *"pain"* exhibits itself as:

- Struggling to **win *"good"* clients**
- Feeling like they're **selling products** rather than ***"providing a service"***
- Spending a lot of money on **marketing**
- Always **competing** for business - but not *"looking different"*

The **Advisor** feels as though they are in a ***"hamster wheel"***

Accountants face very similar problems of *"commoditization,"* which we covered extensively in the ***"Art of Collaboration."***

The majority of Advisors and Accountants (certainly the good ones) understand and recognize that they need to change. However, their key question is **HOW TO CHANGE?**

At Elite (and our associated business – VFO Services), we help Advisors and Accountants to answer that question.

Firstly, we help them to form partnerships, and having done so, work with them to show them **HOW to *"position themselves"*** with their best clients to be able to demonstrate:

- Forward-Looking Approach
    - Helping their clients to achieve their *"big goals"*
- Proactive Style

- Helping their clients make *"smarter decisions"*
- Helping their clients to protect and grow their wealth

- **Wider Focus – *"Holistic and Comprehensive Advice"***
  - Helping their best clients - who want:
    - Broader scope of services (not just traditional financial planning)
    - Integrated strategic advice across a wide spectrum
  - They don't want to be *"stuck in narrow advisory silos"*

Financial Advisors need to understand the shifting needs of clients in a rapidly changing market. They need to be aware of the ***"BLAC grid"*** to track changing client perceptions. Where ***"BLAC"*** stands for:

- **B**latant: Is their frustration **obvious?**
- **L**atent: Is their frustration **hidden or emerging?**
- **A**spirational: Is solving their frustration a ***"nice to have"*?**
- **C**ritical: Is solving their frustration **urgent?**

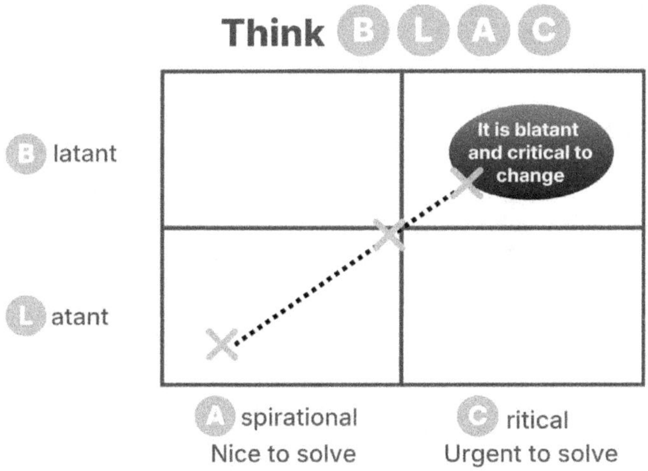

It's not acceptable for Financial Advisors or Accountants to be complacent about their clients in terms of:

- Their frustrations being only **Latent**
- Their desire for change as merely **Aspirational**

Your best clients are no longer positioned in the bottom left quadrant of the above *"BLAC"* grid.

Today, your wealthy and successful clients are firmly in the top right quadrant. Their frustrations with professional Advisors and Accountants are both **Blatant** and **Critical**. Their need for change and a better professional advice service has become urgent.

This book will open the door to change and a better, more proactive, holistic and comprehensive service.

Our Promise to You

We understand that the idea of building profitable and sustainable partnerships with Accountants might seem attractive in theory but, perhaps, unrealistic in practice. We want to reassure you, you are in experienced and capable hands, and the time you invest in reading this book will be well-spent. To demonstrate that experience, we'd like to briefly share our backgrounds and qualifications to help you understand why (working together) we are uniquely able to provide you with valuable insights and advice.

We have written this book to share our knowledge and experience with you. We promise that, within these pages, you will find the tools and strategies you need to overcome the challenges facing advisors today. We understand the *"pain points"* and frustrations that advisors face with the *"commoditization"* of services to the pressure of the *"hamster wheel"* and the *"boiling frog"* syndrome. We've both been there *"in the trenches,"* and, together, we know how to help you escape these traps.

Welcome and Introductions

Anton Anderson

As a natural-born entrepreneur with a passion for business and finance, I've always been drawn to financial advising. I began my career at Smith Barney but soon realized I wanted a more boutique-firm environment. I joined a multi-disciplinary firm in San Diego that offered financial, estate, and tax planning. In 2009, I started my own practice, initially growing it through buying leads, hosting dinner seminars, and radio advertising. After a year, I longed to return to a multi-discipline approach, collaborating with other professionals to grow my practice.

Over the next four years, I embarked on a journey of learning how to work with Accountants, Attorneys, and other niche specialists participating in nearly a dozen different training programs.

By 2012, things started to click, and my practice grew rapidly by building strategic partnerships with Accountants. We used what we called a "Team Based Model" rather than the traditional-referral partnerships that were prevalent at the time. This "team" approach really allowed us to leverage each other's strengths while mitigating our weaknesses.

In 2014, I exited my individual practice and co-founded Elite Resource Team. The mission was to take what we had learned and help financial advisors differentiate themselves in a crowded and competitive market. As a Consultant, Investor, and Thought Leader, I have trained over 1,200 Advisors across forty states, teaching them how to build Accountant partnerships and leverage the power of a Virtual Family Office. I have also co-authored two Amazon bestselling books on related topics, *"The Art of Collaboration"* and *"The Art of Proactivity."*

Paul Latham

When I moved to the USA in late 2011, I originally decided to return to a *"former business love,"* which was **strategic business advisory**. This was a talent I developed when I was at Lathams Chartered Accountants in the UK, and which we covered extensively in the *"Art of Proactivity."*

After moving to the USA, I firmly believed that there was a huge opportunity to replicate what we had achieved at Lathams Accountants, by joining forces with ambitious Accountant firms (with the aim to disrupt the USA accounting market). HaydenRock Solutions was originally created with that disruption in mind.

However, as explained in the *Art of Collaboration*, during the HaydenRock journey, I joined forces with Anton Anderson at Elite, where we now work, with both Accountants and Financial Advisors (often both together in collaboration).

In this book, we focus on how Advisors can build partnerships with Accountants. In particular, I look at this from the perspective of the Accountant, what they are thinking, and how they will benefit from the partnership they create with the Advisor.

As I said in the *"Art of Running a Virtual Family Office,"* this journey feels like I have gone *"full circle."* From training to become a Chartered Accountant (like a CPA in UK) in the early *"eighties"* to helping build and grow Lathams in the *"nineties"* to selling it for

$45m in 2001.[1] Today at Elite, I increasingly find myself *"joining the dots"* between past, present, and future.

It's an exciting time for both Advisors and Accountants, as the industry is continuing to change, and the opportunities to build partnerships and differentiate themselves in the marketplace have never been better!

Elite Resource Team and Virtual Family Office Services

Before we get into the details of the book, we need to explain the relationship between Elite and VFO Services (and the reason why Anton and Paul founded VFO Services).

Elite Resource Team was the original **Member Training Business** for the Team Based Model. We previously explained in the ***"Art of Collaboration"*** how the **Team Based Model** worked, and how that was hugely beneficial for Advisors (and Accountants) who were **willing to put in the *"hard yards"*** to **integrate the model** into their business.

However, Anton and Paul recognized the need for a **faster and easier solution** that was particularly aimed at the needs of already successful, busy Advisors who **wanted to grow revenues via Accountant Partnerships** and wanted a simple *"turnkey"* solution.

Most busy and successful Advisors simply do not have the time to spend months and years ***"mastering the rules like a pro"*** as required to be able to put the Elite learning around building accountant partnerships into practice and *"do-it-themselves."*

Those Advisors could immediately see the **benefit to ADVISORS** of Accountant Partnerships. They could see how working with Accountants would help them reach more clients (of the *"right type"*) and generate more revenue as a result.

However, where they previously struggled was to be able to offer Accountants something valuable in return. In short, what was the **benefit to the ACCOUNTANT** (beyond the Advisor service itself)?

Let's face it, it is hard for Accountants to get too excited about a typical Advisor's ***"commodity service,"*** especially when they probably have other Advisors referring work to them and competing for their attention. Essentially, the Accountant is the *"pretty girl at the bar,"* asking the Advisor, *"so, tell me what makes you special"*?

Anton and Paul recognized that Advisors needed help with two things.

- **Offer Accountants something different and valuable**
  - Providing a tangible benefit to Accountant
    - Help **initiate the partnership** with Accountant

- **Offer Accountants an easy way to *"monetize the relationship"***
  - Without the Advisor needing to train the Accountant
    - Help **sustain the partnership** with Accountant

Anton and Paul wanted to be able to help Advisors offer both of the above to the Accountant, whilst recognizing there must be ***"no hard yards"*** required from the Advisor or Accountant in doing so.

In our sister publication, ***"The Science of Running a Virtual Family Office,"*** we described Anton and Paul's initial *"ah-hah moment,"* and when their idea of VFO Services was first conceived (from the viewpoint of helping the Advisor clients directly, using VFO Fast Track).

However, having founded VFO Services with that above benefit in mind, that also led Anton and Paul to be able to quickly and easily address both of the Advisor needs highlighted above – but, critically, by approaching the process from both the Advisor and Accountant perspectives.

- VFO Services – running a **VFO Fast Track for the Accountant**
    - Offers something **different and valuable to Accountant**
        - **Monetizes the relationship** for Accountant
        - As well as Advisor – where compliance allows

Anton and Paul also understood a **second and critical part of the required game-plan** (again concentrating on Accountant perspective).

The Team Based Model works best when either the Advisor or Accountant (or both) is able to create a business structure that we call ***"Two Businesses Under One Roof."***

This ***"second business structure"*** concept was discussed at length in the ***"Art of Proactivity"*** (where Paul described the growth of Lathams Accountants).

Focusing on the needs of Accountants (but just like Advisors), they have a predominantly ***"commodity business"*** (in their case it is tax compliance).

Accountants need to create ***"Two Businesses Under One Roof,"*** which follows an understanding that they have a clear and fundamental need to **SEPARATE** their traditional **compliance** business from a **planning** business.

Let us explain further. Accountants almost always have a traditional core business (specific services will vary by Accountant and include other areas like books and records), typically ***"Tax Compliance"*** work.

The first goal of any Accountant is to **grow that core business** (Accountants reading this, please don't misunderstand the point we are making. We 100 percent know your commodity service also provides value) – and might be best expressed as:

- **Goal 1** – *"Grow tax compliance - be **efficient and scalable**"*

However, Accountants also increasingly recognize a further need to **differentiate** and **add further value via proactive planning service.**

- **Goal 2** – *"Proactive planning to support best clients"*
    - Who require more complex planning services

It should be obvious that to totally integrate both goals into a single business entity would be confusing. We would see problems like:

- Charging fees for Goal 1 that also somehow cover Goal 2
    - Different team members servicing both goals
        - This problem is further exacerbated once you recognize that not every client wanting core services will also need or want planning services.

- Recognizing Accountants want to maximize profit in both areas
    - How you achieve that is radically different in each area

In fact, the reason why problems happen is the **lack of clear separation between Goal 1 and Goal 2** (but with appropriate client connection to the *"boutique"* as shown by the arrow in the illustration below).

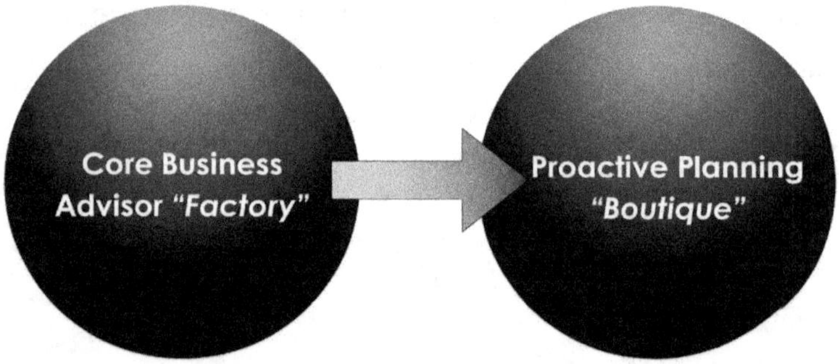

When an Accountant **does not separate,** as shown above, their **value proposition likely becomes *"confusing and jumbled"*** to their client.

- For example, in a proactive planning business, it is highly appropriate to describe your team's *"holistic and proactive"* approach.
    - However, those words are not required and not appropriate when talking purely about the core accountant business
        - When operating in a compliance *"silo"* – and not *"holistic"* by definition

Key Difference between Goal 1 and Goal 2 at a High Level

- **Compliance Business** – focused mostly on **EFFICIENT** delivery
  - Think of this like the Accountants *"factory"*
    - Grow by increasing volume of (example) tax compliance
- **Planning Business** – focused on **VALUE ADDED** delivery
  - Think of this like their *"planning boutique"*
    - Grow by adding value and solving complex problems

It is very hard for an individual Accountant to *"straddle"* both of the above simultaneously (without *"hands-on"* help).

As Paul Latham described in the ***"Art of Proactivity,"*** for an individual Accountant to try to do both (without separation) generally results in ***"Monday to Friday syndrome."***

"On Monday I will be efficient –
and on Tuesday I will add value –
and on Wednesday I will be efficient –
and on Thursday I will add value –
and by Friday . . ."

By Friday, Accountants are most likely not maximizing performance in either area.

To maximize the probability of success and to make this second planning business easy for Accountants to implement was the secondary reason why VFO Services was created by Anton and Paul.

- VFO Services allows Accountants to ***"bolt-on their Planning Boutique"***
- VFO Services does all the ***"heavy lifting."*** It provides:
  - Value Proposition – to win new work
  - *"Front of House"* Planning Team – facilitate the client discussion
  - *"Behind the Scenes"* - Planning Team - liaison with VFO Specialists
  - Efficient administration, billing and client communication
- Accountant is positioned as ***"trusted client relationship lead"*** – where their main role is purely to ***"hand-hold"* client**

The introduction of VFO Fast Track for Accountants provided an easy answer to their conundrum, and at the same time, allows the Advisor to ***"gift them the solution"*** – by helping them to offer Accountants a true benefit and the ability to monetize the partnership.

It was clear to Anton and Paul that VFO Services was going to provide a winning formula for those busy Advisors who wanted to form accountant partnerships and simultaneously offer Accountants something of true value.

VFO Services was a ***"game changer."***

Having explained the above, it is time to move to Part 2 and focus on the specific type of Advisor you are.

PART 2

What Type of Financial Advisor Are You?

Advisors Require a *"Compliance Driven"* Vision

Very simplistically, there are **three broad types of Financial Advisor**:

Those who have a vision to offer wider advice to their best clients (via the Virtual Family Office) – and are:

1. **Not overly constrained** by compliance factors.
2. **Somewhat constrained** by compliance factors.
   Can offer wider advice via VFO but cannot accept revenue share from VFO Specialists
3. **Very constrained** by compliance factors:
   Cannot offer wider advice via VFO regardless of revenue share arrangements

At Elite and VFO Services, we have different *"Fast Track"* type solutions for each of the above types of Financial Advisor.

If you are Financial Advisor **type 1** above or possibly **type 2,** you should start with our separate book:

- ***"The Science of Running a Virtual Family Office"***
  - Working with **VFO Fast Track**

However, if you are the Financial Advisor **type 3** or possibly **type 2**, then this book is the best starting point for you.

- ***"The Science of Building Accountant Partnerships"***
  - Working with **Partnership Fast Track**.

Two Things to Know About Fast Track

Whichever book you are reading, there are two key things to know about the ***"VFO Services - Fast Track"*** offerings, they are both:

- **Fast**
  - Designed to **achieve fast results**
- On a **Track**
  - Process driven, and designed to make them **easy to implement**

PART 3

Partnership Fast Track Executive Summary

Partnership Fast Track has an overarching goal to secure for the Advisor 1 or 2 Accountant Partnerships in 90 days or less

It is a "done-with-you" program designed to help you secure (as a minimum goal) your first signed Accountant Partnership within 90 days.

We don't just train Advisors, we actually attend the meetings with Accountants and Advisors, facilitate and lead the conversations, and help close the deal.

CONSISTENT MEASURABLE RESULTS

40%

Of accountants we meet with will sign an agreement

81 DAYS

Average time from starting Partnership Fast Track to securing your first accountant signed engagement agreement

There is a key point implicit in the above – **you will need to invite Accountants to the program** – because we don't stop after training!

However, rest assured, we provide all the scripts, so you will know what to say. The key point being that at Elite and VFO Services we focus on what we call the ***"three ingredients of business success,"*** which are:

- **Vision** x **Plan** x **Desire** = **Business Success**

We help you achieve your **VISION** and we are "hands-on" in implementing the **PLAN**, but Advisors must bring *"some"* **DESIRE** to help us achieve results for you too!

Partnership Fast Track – Five Step Process

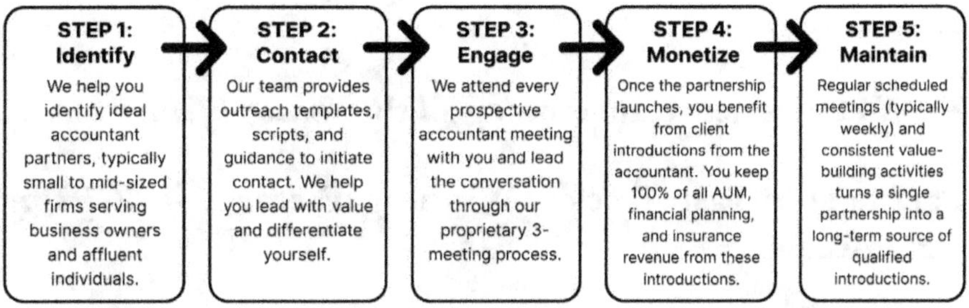

Two Winning Factors as Key Elements of Partnership Fast Track

Partnership Fast Track - Winning Factor 1 – Engage Step 3

The first winning factor – and difference maker is the **Engage** step (step 3 above). That's the ***"done-for-you"*** and ***"hands-on"*** part with the Accountant.

The main reason that the results (shown above) are so quick and consistent is because the VFO Services Team are **already trained and practiced.**[2] They are *"slick and professional,"* which means that all you have to do is follow the Facilitator lead (Advisor has minimal scripted involvement) as they take the Accountant through a **three-meeting process.**

The three-meeting process has been carefully designed to move at the Accountant's pace. We are not rushing them in any way.

Remember, we are working here for the benefit of Accountants (which will ultimately benefit the Advisor), and if you try to *"short-cut"* the process, you will simply *"scare off"* most Accountants (to coin a phrase, *"Advisors are from Mars, and Accountants are from Venus."* Accountants move at their pace, not your pace!).

The **VFO Services team is doing all the *"heavy lifting"* for you.**

Partnership Fast Track - Winning Factor 2 – *"Gifting"* VFO Access

The second winning factor is the ability to offer Accountant access to a **Virtual Family Office** (VFO) once they sign up.

A VFO brings together professionals across multiple disciplines as shown below.

Those different **VFO Specialists** are **collaborating** with **Accountants and their Clients** in a **virtual environment** to deliver comprehensive, coordinated, proactive advice. We discuss the VFO in more detail in the next chapter, but it's the same concept as the family offices used by billionaire families like the Rockefellers (starting in the nineteenth century) through to the examples like the Waltons (just as applicable today in the twenty-first century).

The key difference is the word ***"virtual"*** that makes the traditional family office accessible a winner for the best Accountant types (see below for ideal accountant types).

Elite Resource Team (ERT) is North America's largest Virtual Family Office provider, serving more than 1,200 Financial Advisors and Accountants nationwide.[3] The VFO enables Advisors and Accountants to offer billionaire-level family office services to their clients through our extensive team of over seventy-five vetted specialists. However, rather than requiring "billionaire" clients, the VFO serves the more typical, *"mass-affluent," "high-net-worth,"* and successful business owner clients.

As you read this book, you will quickly understand that via Partnership Fast Track, the **Advisor is providing Accountants with a recurring annual *"gift"*** (via a membership discount) to gain access to the Virtual Family Office.

Partnership Fast Track Program includes:

- **Condensed Training**
  - Elite traditionally provided more than eighty hours of content to learn and use - in a *"DIY"* style – with your clients.

    - Partnership FT condenses that to only **three hours of training**

- **Proprietary Email Templates and Meeting Scripts**
  - Proven scripts to get Accountants excited to meet you
    - Set up Accountant meetings
    - Introduce VFO Services to the Accountant

- **VFO Services Facilitates Accountant Discussions**
  - You introduce VFO Services – they lead the presentations
    - Practiced and professional
    - Handle objections
    - Do all the ***"heavy lifting"***

- **Accountant Accessing the Virtual Family Office**
  - VFO Services **provide the gateway** to more than seventy-five professional VFO Specialists – across all five areas
    - Vetted and highly skilled
    - Revenue sharing agreements in place
    - Discounted access for Accountant

Ideal Accountants for Partnership Fast Track

- Ideal ultimately for **VFO Fast Track for Accountants**

The Partnership Fast Track program works best with certain types of Accountants, covering a number of different factors as follows:

- **Accountant Business Ownership Structure**
    - Solo owner firms are perfect
    - Small partnerships work well (one to three partners preferred)
    - Smaller firms can:
        - Move faster/ adapt better / decisions made quicker
- **Firm Size and Agility**
    - Lean, nimble firms, outperform larger firms (at least early on)
    - Avoid firms with more than five Partners / larger teams (typically slow to pivot)
    - Smaller firms have a greater need for VFO
        - Makes them "*look bigger*" and better resourced to their best clients
- **Team Support**
    - Important to have some team support (one or two minimum team)
    - Building ***"two businesses under one roof"*** – team support is important

        - Partner can delegate to team - operational tasks in the "*factory*"
        - Partner can focus more on proactive planning in the "*boutique*"

As well as the above ***"structural"* factors**, we also consider carefully the following:

- **Client Mix**
    - **Quality** matters more than quantity
    - Ideal firms have a good mix of:
        - **Successful Business Owners** (ideally more than 20 percent of clients)
            - *Need to be more than $1 million annual revenues as a minimum*
            - *Not "hobby" or "lifestyle" businesses*
        - **High Net Worth or Mass-Affluent Individuals**
            - *These are a primary focus area*

- **Client Numbers**
    - **Quality** matters more than quantity (see above profiling)
    - Ideal firms have fifty to one hundred target clients
        - Far more attractive than hundreds of low-level W2 clients

- **Accountant Age**
    - Ideal age range is normally thirty-five to sixty
    - Younger accountants often lack a developed client base

    - Older accountants are often more focused on exit planning
        - We want them focused on growth and innovation, not retirement
    - Exceptions obviously exist
        - Above profile usually aligns best with partnership goals

- **Accountant *"Personality"* Type**
    - Ideal Accountant is **open to change**
        - Not stuck in a *"backwards looking"* mindset
    - Ideal Accountant is **highly respected, trusted** by their best clients
        - Want an Accountant where clients take their advice

The last section above about Accountant *"personality"* type are the factors we look at the most in Partnership Fast Track, as well as the crucial client mix and numbers (which are obviously essential and a prerequisite to make VFO Fast Track worthwhile for them and their clients).

If Accountants don't have the ***"right clients"*** combined with the ***"right trusted client relationships"*** and the ***"right attitude to change,"*** we will likely advise to stop the process with that Accountant after Meeting 1 in the Engage process.

We take account of all the factors outlined above, but the above paragraph covers the most important points we look for.

Tips for Success in Partnership Fast Track Program

Our most successful Advisors demonstrate some common traits which are detailed below:

- **Commitment and Mindset**
  - Typically, two hours per week
    - Initially in training
    - Then introducing clients to process
  - Designed for busy Advisors
    - ***"Consistency beats intensity"***

- **Follow the Process**
  - Called *"Fast Track"* for a reason!
    - Our three-meeting process enjoys a high close rate
    - ***"Trust the process – it works"***

- **Use the Scripts**
  - Our scripts are tried – tested – and proven!
    - ***"Don't be tempted to reinvent the wheel"***

- **Target the *"Right"* Accountants**
  - Look for Accountants with successful business owners (as best clue)
    - Fitting the ideal accountant descriptions above
    - ***"Accountants open to change and collaboration"***

- ***Allow VFO Services to Lead Meetings***
    - Show up prepared – and introduce us
        - VFO Services handle the majority of presentation
        - ***"Your only job is show up and be prepared"***

- **Leverage the VFO Services Team**
    - The team are committed to making this a success for you
        - ***"Let them do the heavy lifting"***

- **Fully Leverage the VFO**
    - This is the **KEY BENEFIT** Advisors bring to Accountants
        - Don't think that *"asking nicely"* will be sufficient
        - ***"Bring them something they need and will value"***

- **Stay Active in the Elite Community**
    - All our Advisors have been where you are at one time (just starting)
        - Collaborate with successful advisors – and learn from them
        - ***"Success is literally at your fingertips"***

Compensation Structure from Partnership Fast Track

Compensation arising from the Accountant Partnership – whether directly with the Accountant, or via VFO Fast Track for Accountants will obviously vary depending upon your compliance type.

All Advisor Types (Types 1-2-3 as described in Part 2)

Advisors will always retain **100 percent of revenue from all regulated activities**, to include:

- Assets Under Management (AUM) fees
- Financial Planning fees
- Life Insurance commissions
- Annuity commissions
- All other securities and traditional insurance product compensation

There is no revenue sharing arrangement on securities transactions, traditional insurance products, or advisory services with Elite Resource Team or VFO Services. Note - some advisors do have revenue share arrangements with the Accountants on the activities, but that is strictly between the Advisor and Accountant.

The above generally is where Accountants introduce their clients to the Advisor in what might be described as the traditional, or *"normal way"*, as a result of your collaboration.

Advisor Type 1 (and possibly Type 2)

VFO Specialist revenues, for services outside the Advisor's core offering, are **shared with the Accountant and Advisor where compliance allows.**

Where compliance doesn't allow the Advisor to take a revenue share, then the revenue share would be for the benefit of the Accountant (part of the benefit you are bringing them).

A key factor is that **VFO Services** are **only remunerated upon Accountant success** (as well as working towards the success of their client and with VFO Specialists).

VFO Services are incentivized to ***"make this process work"*** for Accountants (and Advisors where allowed) – their clients – the VFO Specialists – as well as ourselves. Our goal is truly to create a ***"win-win-win-win"*** **scenario for all stakeholders.**

Summary Benefits of Using Partnership Fast Track

If we make a comparison between the traditional Advisor situation (where they are working alone) and building Accountant Partnerships:

- **Without Accountant Partners** versus working **with Partners**

    - Spend too much money on marketing
        - **Now near zero marketing costs**

- Constantly pursue *"cold prospects"*
  - **Warm introductions from trusted source**

- Low close rates (typically 10 percent to 20 percent)
  - **Significantly higher close rates** (typically 70 percent to 80 percent)[4]

- Advisor stuck on the *"marketing hamster wheel"*
  - **Working on *"autopilot"*** (goal of one or two new clients per week)[5]

"Two Elephants in the Room" (overcome by Partnership Fast Track)

There are two final *"elephants in the room"* when talking about building Accountant Partnerships, that Partnership Fast Track helps you overcome.

"Elephant 1" – Accountant's Hidden Worry

When Advisors normally approach Accountants, the Accountant will likely have some **unspoken fears** (that they rarely say *"out loud"* to the Advisor).

Accountants will likely be thinking about concerns like:

- *"I can't introduce client X – they were referred to me by Advisor A"*
- *"I can't introduce client Y – I already introduced to Advisor B"*

- *"I can't introduce client Z – I know they are really happy with Advisor C"*

Accountants get stuck with worrying about the clients they cannot introduce (probably rightly), rather than thinking about their fiduciary duty and the benefit they can bring to all their other clients. However, the result is often that the potential Accountant Partnership is doomed from the start – and Accountants just *"ghost"* the Advisors – as the conversation feels too difficult.

The reality is that **no Accountant is likely to be able to introduce 100 percent of all their clients to any particular Advisor**. That is a fact (almost always), and Advisors need to get used to that reality.

VFO Services tackles that first *"elephant"* head on in the meetings (Accountants think quietly *"phew"*), and in fact **VFO Services existence is the answer to Accountants problem** (described above).

Precisely **because** Accountants are also **working with VFO Services** via **VFO Fast Track for Accountants** (alongside the partnership with Advisor), the VFO Services Facilitator can reassure the Accountant and address their fears.

- *"No, you will not be 'tied-at-the-hip' to the Advisor on every case"*
    - Where appropriate introduce the Advisor
        - who needs the service of a good Financial Advisor
    - Where conflicted – Advisor will not be in meeting with the client
        - it will only be Accountant and VFO Services team
        - The client will still receive the benefit of VFO

It should also be noted that (where compliance allows) VFO Services will pay the Advisor 10 percent of VFO Revenues they generate from Accountant clients even where Advisor was not involved.

- Advisor receives primary benefit of Accountant Partnership
    - Introductions to clients for their *"core business"* (AUM etc.)

- Advisor receives secondary benefit of Accountant Partnership
    - Revenue shares from VFO (where compliance allows)
        - Even where they are not involved directly

"Elephant 2" – Advisor's Practical Concern

This one is really simple. At Elite we have two types of Accountant / Advisor Partnerships.

- **VFO Associate Accountant**
    - This is where Advisor trains Accountant in VFO process
    - Advisor facilitates the client discussions

- **VFO Fast Track Accountant**
    - This is where VFO Services train Accountants
    - VFO Services facilitates their client discussions

VFO Associate Accountant Route

This is most appropriate where Elite have trained a very large and successful Advisor practice, and they have **"learned the Team Based Model rules like a pro."** They have the **bandwidth and wider team resources**, as well as the **desire to service Accountants clients directly** and **without VFO Services involvement**.

That is totally fine (*"great"* in fact), but the reality is that those **Advisors must do all the *"heavy lifting."*** With the typical smaller Advisor (even where they have learned the rules and have desire), they are **limited to the number of Accountants with whom they can form a partnership**. Generally, unless they are a heavily resourced Advisor and team, that may mean only two or three Accountant Partnerships is practical.

The Advisor has to navigate *"Elephant in the Room 1"* above.

This route is clearly totally inappropriate for Advisor Compliance Type 3 (and maybe Type 2 also) as discussed in Part 2.

VFO Fast Track for Accountant Route

By contrast, this route is most appropriate where Advisor:

- Doesn't have time or desire to *"learn the rules like a pro"*
- Doesn't want to train Accountants in Team Based Model
- Doesn't want to facilitate every single client meeting
- Especially where the client is not interested in financial advice
- Doesn't want to do all the *"heavy lifting"*

Instead, the Advisor does want to:

- Enjoy the benefits of the Partnership for **traditional Advisor work flows**
    - Particularly for compliance reasons
- Enjoy the benefits of **VFO Revenues**
    - Where compliance allows
- Allow the Accountant to **escape *"Elephant 1"***
    - Not make Accountant feel *"joined at the hip"* to Advisor
- Enjoy the benefit of **limitless numbers of Accountant Partnerships**
    - Because they are not training / facilitating every meeting

It is safe to say that, since the introduction of VFO Services, **the vast majority of busy Advisors** (who are properly advised by a coach that truly understands what they are doing) – **chooses VFO Fast Track for Accountants Route the vast majority of the time.**

The majority of Advisors don't even entertain the VFO Associate Accountant Route. Bluntly, they have better things to do with their time (and don't even want to offer that option to any Accountants they meet via Partnership Fast Track). In that circumstance, Accountants can generally be placed with a different Advisor who does like doing all the *"heavy lifting."*

PART 4

Understanding the Virtual Family Office

Origins of a Family Office

Once upon a time, there was the Rockefeller Family.

We gave you an overview of this in Part 3, but given the importance of the VFO to most Accountants that you will be seeking to gain partnerships with, it's important for you to have a more detailed understanding of the concept. Let's start by taking you back in time, to 1882.

That was when the Rockefeller Family first created the concept of a *"Family Office."*

The Rockefeller Family were frustrated because they had numerous and various professional specialists, but they were **providing conflicting advice** to the family.

The Rockefellers **decided to make a change**. They interviewed dozens of professionals to find the best of the best, and then offered to hire them to work exclusively as their full-time employees.

The goal was to create a team that could provide the family with the **best holistic advice and the best possible outcomes and solutions.**

This *"Family Office"* concept quickly caught on with other wealthy families.

The idea of a Family Office was a great benefit to ultra wealthy families, but it was obviously not an option for more *"normal high net worth"* people because of the huge cost of employing teams of professionals and specialists.

Jumping from the nineteenth century, modern day twenty-first century family offices are still used by ultra-high net worth families, including those shown below.

Kylie Jenner
Cosmetics/Celebrity
Net Worth: $700M+
Est. Cost: $1-3M

Michael Jordan
Basketball Legend
Net Worth: $3.2B
Est. Cost: $5M-$15M

Jeff Bezos
Amazon
Net Worth: $250B
Est. Cost: $350M

Walton Family
Walmart
Net Worth: $250B
Est. Cost: $350M-$500M

However, the internet and the virtual world has removed the obstacle of cost (of using a family office) completely.

Birth of the Virtual Family Office

The internet has been a game-changer

Today at Elite (and for Accountants working with VFO Services), the *"Virtual Family Office"* uses the same foundational concept as a traditional

Family Office, which is to have **specialists across five broad professional disciplines**, which are:

- Advanced Tax Planning,
- Wealth Management
- Legal Services
- Business Advisory
- Risk Mitigation

The VFO specialists all collaborate with our trained professional Members (including Accountants) in a virtual environment to **deliver that proactive, holistic, and comprehensive advice to successful clients.**

Effectively, the VFO provides a **wider resource to serve client needs.**

The five areas (detailed above) are obviously extremely diverse, and it would be impossible for most individual professional firms to be able to offer true expertise and specialist help across all of them.

Elite has spent a decade building their VFO and is comprised of more than seventy-five individual ***"VFO Specialists."*** Elite and VFO Services also have a full time employee (called a "*VFO Liaison*") whose only job is to manage the relationships with these specialists and help professionals in the Elite Community to become comfortable and work with them effectively with their clients.

To allow easy access to the VFO, we create a **Team-Based Model** structure that looks like the illustration below, where, as you can see that model is comprised of **two collaborative teams:**

- **Proactive Planning Team**
- **Virtual Family Office Specialists**

Both teams are important in terms of **providing the holistic and comprehensive service** needed to best service clients.

We go into more detail in Part 8 - when we talk about how the Accountant will work with their clients to ***"monetize"*** the relationship.

PART 5

Identify Target Accountants

As we outlined in Part 3, we use a five-step process in Partnership Fast Track, which is shown below. Let's start by taking you through Step 1: identify.

We previously covered in Part 3 the key attributes of the ideal target accountant. To remind you those attributes may be summarized as:

"Right type of clients"

The first pre-requisite is they appear to have the *"right type of clients"* – both in terms of mix and quantity. The reason that we consider them *"right"* is because these are the three types that offer the most opportunity working with the Virtual Family Office.

- ***"Mass-Affluent"***
  - Annual Income – typically more than $250,000
  - Assets – typically more than $500,000 (excluding home)
- ***"High-Net-Worth"***
  - Annual Income – will vary by region across different parts of USA
  - Assets – starting point $1 million (excluding home)
- **"Successful" Business Owner**
  - Annual Revenue – minimum $1 million (ideally more)
  - *"Proper Business"* – with *"desire to grow"* not *"lifestyle"* / *"hobby"*

"Right Personality"

This section can really be sub-divided into two attributes – they are **open to change** and are **highly respected and trusted** by their clients.

- **Accountant *"Personality"* Type**
    - Ideal Accountant is **open to change**
        - Not stuck in a *"backwards looking"* mindset
    - Ideal Accountant is **highly respected, trusted** by their best clients
        - Want an Accountant where clients take their advice

These attributes are crucial – as well as other – *"nice to have"* factors like business structure, number of partners, age etc., if Accountants don't have the ***"right clients,"*** combined with the ***"right trusted client relationships"*** and the ***"right attitude to change,"*** we will likely advise to stop the process with that Accountant after Meeting 1 in the Engage process.

So, how do you identify them?

Firstly, give yourself a good statistical chance of success. This is a *"numbers game"* and not a *"single rifle shot"* (unless you are feeling lucky!).

You should start by building a *"long-list"* of maybe thirty to fifty potential targets. In part, that is to create the best statistical chance of success, but it is also to stretch your thinking and to not settle for *"mediocre,"* but aim for *"great potential partnerships with Accountants."*

Top ways to identify potential target accountants include the following:

- **Talking to current prospects and clients**
- **Warm non-client relationships**
- **Old fashioned networking**

- **LinkedIn organic**

At Elite, we go into detail to teach some of these approaches in more detail (see illustrated examples below).

Client/Prospect Accountant Discussion

How do your taxes get done?

- If Accountant, ask about the relationship
- Great, average, poor
  - Great and average = Intro for you
  - Poor = Needs new Accountant

Asking clients for Intro to Great & Average Accountants:

> "I'd like to shoot you an email as soon as we get off the phone, and I'd ask that you forward that email to your Accountant and include me on it. This is important because some of the planning that my team and I are going to look at should be discussed with your Accountant to make sure that there's nothing that we suggest that conflicts with what they are looking at doing this year. Also, based on what you've told me about your Accountant, I may have a few other clients that are a good fit for them. Does that sound fair enough?"

Warm Non-Client Contacts

"Warm Contacts" would include business associates (business brokers, business appraisers, property and casualty agents, bankers, attorneys, coaches, etc), as well as friends and family members.

Share with them:

> "I have been evaluating my client relationships and overall business. It's become clear that numerous changes over the last few years have created a greater need for key advisors to collaborate. There's too much for any one professional in one industry to juggle without the clients suffering. As a result, I'm looking to form two or three key relationships with tax professionals to bring more proactive and holistic planning to mutual clients. What I'd like to do is shoot you an email as soon as we get off the phone, and all I'm going to need you to do is forward that email to your CPA and CC me on that introduction. Does that sound fair enough?"

Networking

CPE Events, Networking Groups, Non-Profits

Not about meeting Accountants but meeting other professionals, then using the warm non-client technique mentioned above.

Be a connector and activate Law of Reciprocity

LinkedIn Organic

Join industry related groups and connect with clients and search their connections

Updated LinkedIn Profile

Name: John/Jane Smith

Title: Team Based Model Consultant

Industry: Financial Services

Background Summary: Use your own background, but make sure to position your experience in a way that shines a light on your work with Accountants and attorneys.

Here is Anton Anderson's background summary, as an example:

Anton began his career in 2003 working for Smith Barney while studying business in college. He graduated from the University of California, Santa Barbara in the top 5 percent of his class, and was honored as the "Student Leader of the Year" by The Society of Leadership and Success. Since graduating, he has developed a diverse and valuable financial background as an investor and advisor, working for both small boutique investment firms, as well as larger financial corporations. Since 2009, he has focused on working with CPAs, helping them offer more proactive and holistic planning to their clients. Anton is a published author, and has worked and/or lived in the United States, Australia, and the United Kingdom. He currently resides in downtown Del Mar, California.

Accountant Websites

Another great way to begin to identify potential targets is to simply look at a number of Accountant websites. These tell you a lot of information very quickly about any Accountant Firm.

You should be able to address certain points very quickly. Factors like:

- **Business structure**
    - Number of Partners
    - Age of Partners
        - The bios usually give you a good idea (when qualified etc.)
    - Size of Team
        - There is usually an *"about us"* section

However, whilst the above are factual and should be easy to spot, there are other clues from their website. Look for things like:

- Does their website look ***"modern"?***
- Does their website look ***"well maintained"?***
    - Look at things like News / Blogs – when was the last time they posted?

- What **services do they offer?**
    - Offer only traditional services – like compliance, books, and records
    - Also, Advisory services – like tax planning, business advisory, etc.

In terms of the last point (about service types), we should expand that discussion further as it has layers of nuance to look for.

If their services look **very traditional,** then you can look at that in two ways:

- Maybe they are *"stuck in the mud"* – that's not so good
- However, it would be easy to *"bolt-on"* a VFO Business with little complication

If their services look **very planning-orientated** (things like pushing tax planning, financial services, business advisory, other niche planning areas), again you can look at that in two ways:

- They likely have the *"right mindset"* – that's great
- However, they may not think they need the VFO quite so much

- Two Important points here on their perception of what they ***"think"* they need.**

- Firstly, from our experience, the biggest value VFO Services bring to accountants is the **IMPLEMENTATION of the VFO**. Many accountants believe they have access to *"everything"* already but struggle actually driving the results (lack of process, lack of training, lack of time, etc.). As powerful as tools or strategies are, they are only valuable if the clients implement the plan!

- Secondly, even if the Accountant has **some** planning resources, they probably won't cover **all the areas of the VFO.** By using the Elite VFO they can tailor their particular VFO to effectively **only add** the VFO Specialist areas that **they don't currently resource.**

As with most things in life, you are **looking for the middle ground**. You want to see:

- Evidence of trying to present as "*forward-thinking*" – that demonstrates the *"right mindset"*
- Evidence that it's *"more what they say – and less what they actually do"*

The best way to check the last bullet is to look at the **bios of the Partner and Team**. What services do they seem to talk about the most?

Often, you will see Accountant websites that try to suggest "*forward-looking*" services, but the **cold, harsh reality is that most likely 90 percent of the work they do is still compliance**. This is perfect because it hints at *"right mindset,"* but that they lack true capability to deliver (and the VFO will help them).

As Paul Latham says, with confidence, when he first meets most smaller accountants (and without knowing them), *"As a smaller firm, you probably have a strength and a weakness."*

- Strength is **close personal contact** with clients
- Weakness is **lack of resources** to solve more complex problems

They usually agree, and we know the VFO will help them. However, the only way we will truly know is to have a conversation and to meet them. First, we will need to invite them (which takes us to Step 2 of the process).

PART 6

Contact Accountants

The reality is that there are many ways to contact target accountants. Here is where we start the coaching at Elite in terms of overview methods available to you:

Overview

- How Do You Contact Them?
- Client Introductions
- Warm Non-Client Introductions
- Tax Season Survival Kits
- Cold Contact Options

Looking in some more detail starting with a third-party introduction, where you provide the introducer with a template email to send to the target (basically making it easy for them).

Advisor Follow-Up Email

Here is the email you'll want to **customize,** then send to your client for them to forward to their Accountant:

> Dear (Accountant's Name),
>
> I hope you're doing well.
>
> I wanted to introduce you to one of my other trusted advisors. (Advisor Full Name). He/She is doing some unique work with Accountants by helping them add value in the way they operate with their clients. We are currently looking at a few ideas that I wanted him/her to run by you.
>
> (Advisor Name) - (Accountant's Name) is an exceptional Accountant and very highly regarded in the community. Please reach out to him/her, so you can get a time to talk on the calendar.
>
> Sincerely,

(Introducing Party's Name)

Once the above has been sent, you (Advisor) then write back immediately along the following lines. The key is to keep it short (Accountants are busy) and make sure you respond first to *"control the narrative."*

Third Party Email to Accountant

After you receive the email, write back with a short recognition such as:

"Thank you _______ (Introducing Party's Name) for the introduction. _______ (Accountant's Name), I look forward to connecting. How does a fifteen-minute call at ____ (time) ____ next (___day___) work for you?"

Warm Non-Client Introduction

As previously mentioned, start by sharing with them:

- You have been evaluating your client relationships and overall business
- Clear that numerous changes over the last few years have created a greater need for key advisors to collaborate
- Too much for any one professional in one industry to juggle without clients suffering
- Looking to form two or three key relationships with tax professionals to bring more proactive and holistic planning to mutual clients

Make it easy for them (and control the variables) by providing a template email for them to send.

Best Practices - Provide Email Template

Example Email:

> Jane - I wanted to introduce a friend/advisor of mine, ______. He/She is doing some unique work with Accountants, helping them add value to the ways they operate with their clients.
>
> ______ - Jane is a well-respected Accountant in the community and a partner at XYZ.
>
> I think it would be worth both of your time to connect. ______, please reach out to Jane, so you can get a call on the calendar.
>
> Best, John

The following is a real-life example (with names changed). Look at how quickly it unfolded – starting at 7:47 a.m. on a Friday.

> **Sent:** Friday, June 19, 7:47 a.m.
>
> Bill,
>
> I wanted to introduce a friend of mine named Travis Smith. He is doing some unique work with Accountants, helping them add value to the ways they operate with their clients.
>
> Travis - Bill is a well-respected Accountant in the community and partner at Williams Accounting Firm.
>
> I think it would be worth both of your time to get

together for lunch. Travis, please reach out to Bill, so you can get a lunch date on the calendar.

Bob

Ideally respond in less than fifteen minutes, but in this case the Advisor responded to the introduction by 10:20 a.m. – and the Accountant's reply was at 11:17 a.m.

Sent: Friday, June 19, 10:20 a.m.

Thank you for the introduction Bob. Bill, I look forward to meeting you.

How about June 30 or July 2?

Have a great day!

– Travis

Sent: Friday, June 19, 11:17 a.m.

Hi Travis,

I'm flexible on Tuesday, June 30.

Thank you.

Bill

You can, then, see below how quickly the date for the meeting was finalized.

Sent: Friday, June 19, 11:25 a.m.

Hi Bill,

Would 12:00 p.m. at Ruth's Chris work okay with you?

Thanks Bill, look forward to meeting you.

–Travis

Sent: Friday, June 19, 11:35 a.m.
That works great– see you then, Travis.

Tax Season Survival Kit (TSSK)

Moving on from warm introductions, you might try the *"Tax Season Survival Kit"* approach to get noticed by an Accountant.

Types of Lumpy Mail

Something unique to get Accountant's attention

- Can use anytime of year, just change theme
- Example, "Holiday Survival Kit"
- Template letters and follow up provided

Here are a few real-life responses to that approach.

Greg Keiper

March 24

I finally "jumped into" the model this week, rather than observing from the sidelines. I delivered my first 5 TSSK's all to cold CPA relationships. I have heard back from 3 of the 5 CPA's (using the TSSK follow up email). I have scheduled time to talk with one of them and the other 2 have requested I meet with them after tax season at the end of April. Anton Anderson, thank you for the great model! Bob Coleman thanks for your help, encouragement, and for talking off the sidelines!

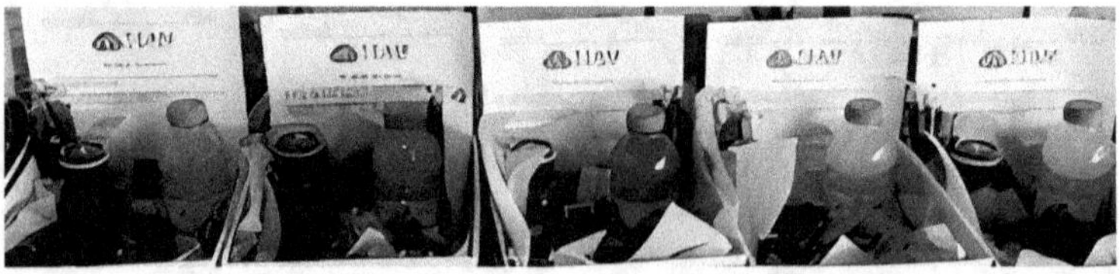

Alexander Skijus

March 23

Delivered another 5 TSSK's today. For all of them, I left the TSSK with the receptionist with a brief description of who I am and why I'm delivering this box. The particular CPA of this story wasn't at the first office location of his firm that I went to today, so I drove 20 miles across town to deliver it to the office location I knew he was at. Bustling office and reception area so I literally only had time to say "hey this is for _______, please tell him I hope he enjoys it and I'll follow up."

I just got a call from the CPA. He was floored (go big or go home with TSSKs). He said it was the nicest thing he's ever recieved. He stopped the whole office and had an employee video him opening the box.

I had my elevator pitch practiced and refined and I nailed it when he asked me what the deal is. He is dying to know more and he kept saying wow... this is what I need, more time and more resources for my 800 business owner clients. His firm has 5000 clients, 800 biz owners.

He thanked me and thanked me and thanked me for the generosity... a favorite item people are enjoying in the kit is a Tide Stin Defender Pen, btw. A member of his staff is calling me tomorrow to schedule a 1st meeting lunch. After an afternoon of obtaining a bit of a headache driving around town, this was the best ending to a day in s while...

LEZGOOO!

Troy Thompson

April 9

TSSK experience.

I delivered 9 TSSK's last Monday and Tuesday. I received 5 responses, all favorable, with 2 appointments scheduled after tax season. I'm working on getting the other 3 to commit to a date.

Cold Accountant Introduction Via Phone

Moving on now to cold calling by phone, here is an example of a good script to follow:

Phone Script:

> Hi, my name is:
>
> I am looking for a fifteen minute call with ______ to go over the type of tax and business planning he/she offers.

The person answering will likely ask questions – and you will reply.

They will then ask you what the appointment will be regarding:

> We work with accountants to help them add value to their clients by leveraging a Virtual Family Office. It would be helpful to know more about the type of advanced tax and business planning you offer to see if you would benefit from a Family Office model.

If pushed for more information again:

> I'm about to jump into another meeting, so I don't have enough time to get into the weeds now, but I'd just be looking to meet with the Accountant for ten minutes or so.

At that point, they're either interested or not. It's typically a quick phone call, so remember "some will, some won't, next." Do not give too much information over the phone, just schedule Meeting #1.

Cold Accountant Introduction Via In-Person

Alternatively, you may drop into the Accountant office and ask for a meeting in person.

Script:

> Hi, my name is _____. I had a meeting down the hall with another Accounting firm and thought I would stop by on my way out to introduce myself. I am looking for a fifteen-minute call to go over the type of tax planning your office offers business owners.

If pushed for more information:

> We work with accountants to help them add value to their clients by leveraging a Virtual Family Office. It would be helpful to know more about the type of advanced tax and business planning you offer to see if you would benefit from a Family Office.

If pushed for more information again:

> Unfortunately, I'm off to another meeting, so I don't have enough time to get into the weeds right now, but I'd just be looking to meet for ten to fifteen minutes.

At that point, they're either interested or not. It's typically a quick visit, so remember "some will, some won't, next."

Cold Accountant Introduction Via Email

Another approach would be to send an email as shown below.

Step 1 - Research

You'll want to build a list of thirty or more accountants (great task for an assistant) and note interesting things they've done or work they've completed.

Step 2 - Write Email

Your goal is to set a ten to fifteen minute phone call (Meeting #1).

> Email Subject: Question About _____ (insert reference to unique item)
>
> Hi, (Accountant's first name)
>
> I came across your blog/article/podcast (try to say something besides website) online titled _____. I found it interesting how you (add something unique about the pieces of info you're referencing, ex. "Broke down your advice into easily understood suggestions").
>
> We work with accountants to help them add value to their clients by leveraging a Virtual Family Office. Based on your website it looks like you are more proactive and value driven than the average Accountant. I'd like to discuss the tax planning you offer your business clients. How would later this week work for a brief conversation?
>
> Best, (Your Name)

Step 3 - Connect on Social Media

In addition to emailing (or something instead of emailing), connect with them on any social media platforms (LinkedIn, Facebook, Instagram, etc.).

Step 4 - Follow Up Call Forty-Eight Hours Later

> Receptionist:
>
> Hi, my name is _____. (Accountant's First Name)'s (Name of article/blog/special report) and would like a ten-minute call to go over the type of tax planning he/she offers.

If pushed for more information:

> We work with accountants to help them add value to their clients by leveraging a Virtual Family Office. It would be helpful to know more about the type of advanced tax and business planning you offer to see if you would benefit from a Family Office model.

If pushed for more information again:

> Unfortunately, I'm off to another meeting, so I don't have enough time to get into the weeds right now, but I'd just be looking to meet with the Accountant for ten minutes or so.

At that point, they're either interested or not. It's typically a quick phone call, so remember *"some will, some won't, next."* Do not give too much information over the phone, just push for the in-person meeting with them.

As Anton likes to say, Step 2 is all about you putting in some *"sweat equity"* to get to the next step, which is **Engage.**

PART 7

Engage with Target Accountants – Meeting #1

Having put in the *"sweat equity"* this is where it gets interesting. As we outlined in Part 3, the Engage step comprises three meetings.

This first meeting is designed to be both relatively brief and *"pacy."*

It is **not a formal presentation,** and we don't use slides, or do any demos (unlike in Meetings 2 and 3).

Using Partnership Fast Track with VFO Services involved, the meetings will always be via **Zoom** (Advisors following the "DIY" approach can choose alternatives like in person or telephone).

The main goal of this meeting is to determine, if they have:

- Right Clients
- Right Client Relationships
- Right Mindset towards change

Below is the **outline agenda** – where, if involved, VFO Services will *"drive,"* including the *"elevator pitch"* and handling objections.

Meeting #1 Prep

What to Say to a Potential Accountant Partner

New Relationship or Resetting Relationship

Meeting Agenda

- Introduction
- Framing Out Meeting
- Diagnostic Questions
- Mission and Purpose
- Summary and Next Steps
- Also discussed:
  Elevator Pitch and Objection Handling

Since there are no slides for Meeting #1, we will share the key parts of the script with you in this book to give you a *"feel"* for the flow and main points.

Introduction

> [ADVISOR SCRIPT] Hi (Accountant Name), I'm (Advisor Name). It's nice to meet you via Zoom. (Pause to let them reply) Let me also introduce a team member of mine that I asked to join us today, (Proactive Facilitator Name).

From here, the advisor can ask a few non-business questions. For example: *How is your week going? Where are you located (small chat about location)? How long have you been working with/known (person that introduced you if applicable)?*

The Advisor will start to *"frame out"* the meeting, before handing over to the VFO Services Proactive Facilitator to handle the rest of the meeting.

Framing Out Meeting

> [ADVISOR SCRIPT] We have found that there are a lot of accountants who are looking to change from the traditional way of doing things - they want to be more "proactive" - more "forward-looking" - add more value to clients and not be tied to the tax season treadmill. The issue is they

are not really sure HOW to make the necessary change or WHO can help them. I asked (PF Name) to join our meeting because he has some unique experience in this regard. (PF Name) can you share a little more about what we've been working on?

[PF TAKES OVER] Absolutely (Advisor Name). So, (Accountant Name) we work with the Team Based Model and help accountants work less and make more by providing proactive and holistic value to clients while improving their work/life balance. In short, we provide:

- Coaching and communities – to help us work collaboratively
- Tools and technology – designed to make life easier
- And most crucially – access to a team of roughly seventy-five national specialists through our Virtual Family Office to help you implement advanced planning solutions

The Proactive Facilitator will then take Accountants through the verbal diagnostic questions. You will see how they tackle the three tests outlined above.

Diagnostic Questions

- *What type of clients do you typically work with?*
- *What percent of your clients would you estimate are mass affluent vs high net worth individuals or business owners?*

- **Test 1:** If 25 percent or more of their clients are "high net worth" or "business owners" then they pass the first test (i.e., they have the "right type of clients").

- *Would you say that most of your clients trust and follow your advice?*
    - **Test 2:** If they say something such as, "yes I think most do" or "I work really hard towards that goal," then they pass the second test (i.e., they have the "right" client relationships).

- *So tell me, where would you like to see your business go in the next twenty-four months?*
    - **Test 3:** Their answer to this question will indicate if they are looking to evolve their practice. Ideally, they mention something about becoming more proactive, offering advisory services, getting away from just charging hourly or per return, etc. If they do indeed want to evolve and grow, then they pass the third test (i.e., they have the "right" attitude).

The Proactive Facilitator would then move towards summarizing.

Summary Statement

Once you are through the questions, you need to diagnose the accountant's situation. Do they, 1) have the "right" type of clients, 2) have the "right" client relationships, and 3) have the "right" attitude to change? If not, politely thank them for their time and let them know that you don't think you'll be able to help them. If they do, then move forward in the script.

Mission and Purpose

Great, that was helpful. Would you like me to tell you a little more about what we do?

So our team provides the coaching, systems, and relationships to empower financial professionals, which is (Advisor's Name) background, tax professionals, which is obviously your background, and a Virtual Family Office, which we help with, to build synergistic partnerships. Together, we form what we call a "proactive planning team" to broaden our capabilities.

The ultimate goal would be to provide clients with a twenty-first century experience through "forward-looking" and added value services.

Summary and Next Steps

If you agree, I'd like to set up two additional meetings, that way we will have plenty of time to get into your specific situation and how this model might help, as well as demo processes and answer any questions you have before deciding whether or not we move forward.

For our second meeting, how does next week look for you? (Schedule day, time, and location). *Great, and then how about the following week for our third meeting?* (Schedule day, time, and location).

Shortly after our meeting, I'm going to send you two calendar invites. Please just accept those on your end once received. Additionally, I'll send a few questions about your practice, we call it the "Accountant Discovery." It will only take about ten minutes to complete and it will really enable us to get the most from our next meeting. That sound fair enough?

End of Meeting

Now that we have *"qualified"* the Accountant, and provided enough information to peak their curiosity, we are ready for Meeting #2.

PART 8

Engage with Target Accountants – Meeting #2

By contrast with Meeting #1, Meeting #2 does involve presenting slides (again via Zoom, assuming VFO Services is involved). It typically takes one hour to complete.

Since the last meeting, Accountant will have completed a simple discovery form (which the team – including Advisor - will have analyzed prior to Meeting #2).

In meeting #2, we will show Accountants how they can increase their revenue by using the VFO and Team Based Model, compared to their traditional model. This is typically achieved by decreasing their low-paying clients (if they choose to), enjoying less stress, and less *"client fatigue," while providing more revenue generating services to their best clients.*

We start by demonstrating that we understand their problems.

The Problem Today

Tax Professionals are expected to do more and more!

The problem is too many clients with low average revenue!

The Math

500 Total Clients
x **$1,000** Per Client

$500,000 Annual Revenue

They have too many clients of the *"wrong type"* – the C or D clients, which compounds and exacerbates other problems as shown below.

Burnout / Work Life Balance	Getting Ideal Clients	Improving Profit Margin
Giving Free Advice	Not Enough/ The Right Staff	Making Enough Money to Retire

What if we approached this problem in a different way? Rather than increasing the number of clients, we decreased the overall number. We focused more on A and B clients, allowing us to dramatically increase the average revenue per client, as well as improve the work/life balance.

Better Math

What if average client revenue was $7,000?

100 A and B Clients
x $7,000 Per Client

$700,000 Annual Revenue

For the moment, without getting stuck on the *"how"* to do it, let's just **look at the new math** if we had 100 A and B clients with an average client revenue of $7,000 per year. As you can see, doing that allows an accountant to work with significantly fewer clients while actually generating $200,000 more in revenue.[6] Not to mention that doing more enjoyable work brings clients more value. And if you're curious where we came up with $7,000 . . . hang tight. We'll show you in a few minutes. For now, does that conceptually make sense?

In the illustration above, we show how fewer clients can easily result in greater revenue for the Accountant. That is simple math for the purposes of this book.

However, the Accountant may want to delve deeper here. For example, they may ask questions like:

- How do you arrive at the answer of $7,000 per client? We cover this in Frequently Asked Questions.
- What happens if I want to introduce your model, but not get rid of 80 percent of my C through F clients? We will also cover this in Frequently Asked Questions.

The goal at this point is to just get the Accountant's attention, and gauge their openness to thinking *"outside the box."* We want them to be open to our perspective that, contrary to popular belief:

- It's not a *"client problem"*
- It's not a *"staffing problem"*
- It's a **MODEL** problem

Once they are willing to accept that possibility, then we can show them a ***"better model."***

The VFO model **builds trust through structure**, not just personality, and gives both Advisors and Accountants what they've been missing, which is **a repeatable way to win – together.**

More than that, it gives the Accountant's better clients what they have been missing, which is **wider and deeper technical resources to help solve more complex problems.**

It results in **shared wins** - for Clients, Accountants, Advisors, Specialists, and, indeed, VFO Services and Elite.

Next Steps

Confirm Meeting #3

During this meeting we will:

- Answer any new **questions** that come up
- Demonstrate the **Proactive Planning Process**
- Discuss ongoing **meetings and training**

Obviously, many Accountants have questions, but again, the Proactive Facilitator is trained to deal with them. Crucially, they drive towards Meeting #3 where most of their detailed questions will be addressed.

PART 9

Engage with Target Accountants - Meeting #3

Again, this presentation is led by the Proactive Facilitator.

We start with an Accountant Revenue Review (driven by the discovery previously provided). We demonstrate how we can help them grow using data we have tracked from hundreds of members. This helps the Accountants get a realistic understanding of the impact this partnership can have on their revenue and work/life balance.

We show them the three big areas where you, as their advisor partner with our support, can help them and provide details on each.

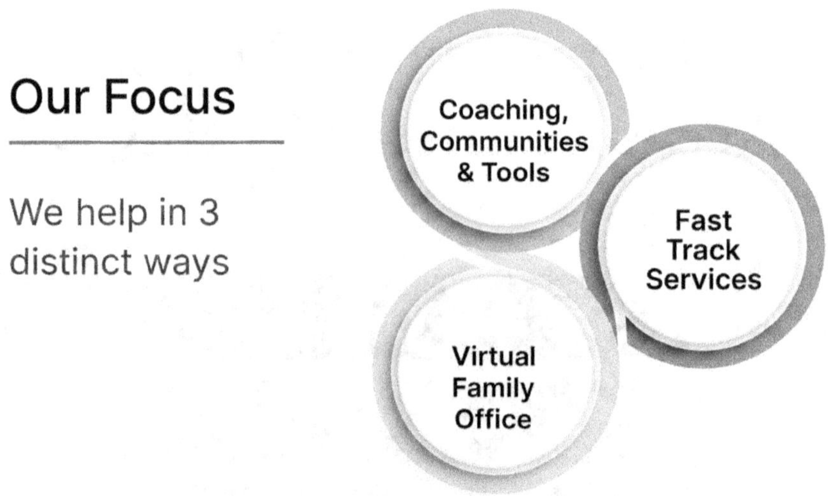

After walking through the three areas we help accountants, we take them through case studies to help "make it real" and provide more insight on how this model works in practice (not just theory).

Having laid the necessary foundation, we will then transition into an overview of the two options they have when working with our model (although many Advisors prefer to only show the VFO Fast Track option – see *"Elephant 2"* in Part 3).

We then focus on VFO Fast Track – showing how there are two broad strands of activity – depending on client needs and preferences.

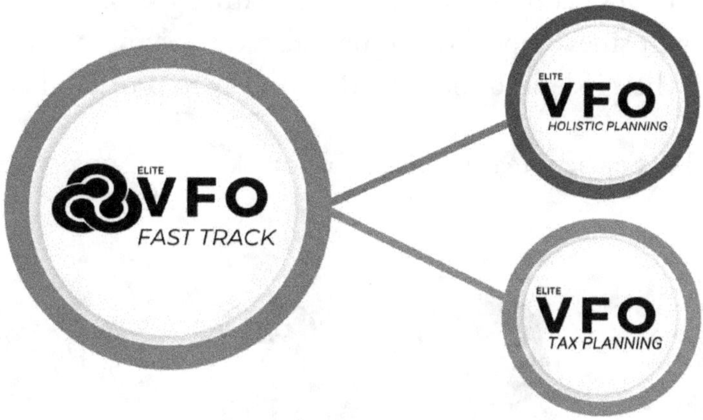

We show them our goal – and later talk through our track record of achieving that.

Goal:

Generate Additional Advisory Revenue in 45 days

We discuss how this ambitious goal is achievable - by leveraging the VFO Services team. They get to essentially *"bolt on"* a proven and turnkey business model onto their already existing practice. This reduces their risks and shortens the runway to profitability.

The VFO Services team consists of four key positions.

Evan Anderson
Proactive Facilitator
Takes clients through process & identifies where they need help

Tracy Miller
VFO Liaison
Helps you and your clients work directly with VFO Specialists

Tim Gacsy
Director of Advanced Tax Planning
Works with VFO Liaison on tax planning options and implications

Team Members
Proactive Coordinator Team
Helps coordinate meetings & track progress

Accountant Investment

If an Accountant attempted to build the VFO Services team on their own, they'd be looking at half a million dollars worth of payroll[7] (not to mention the more than seventy-five VFO Specialists, the software and infrastructure required, and the years of work). That's just one of the reasons why your offer with our team is such a *"no brainer"* for the right Accountants.

VFO Fast Track for Accountants Cost:

- Typically $667 per month
- Reduced to $333 due to Elite Advisor relationship
    - Twelve-month contract
        - Three-month surrender clause

During the meeting, we illustrate their investment – and the $4,000 *"gift"* provided to the Accountant by the Advisor, in terms of discounted membership of VFO Fast Track ($333 x 12 months saving = $4,000).

We compare the above with VFO Associate, which assuming they want it directly (without the Advisor involvement, typically), would cost them $145 per month. For that saving of $188 per month, they receive no training and no access to the VFO Services Team (aside from VFO Liaison). It doesn't take a *"rocket scientist"* to work out which is typically considered the better deal!

VFO Associate Accountant

Cost:

- Typically $145 per month
- Free due to Elite Advisor relationship
- Month to month agreement

Typically at the end of the Meeting, the Accountant makes their final choice, and we deal with their paperwork and onboarding (depending upon choice).

Assuming the Accountant has agreed to *"Engage"* and selected which membership option, we are ready for the *"Monetize"* step of the partnership.

PART 10

Monetize the Relationship[8]

As one of our colleagues, Jon Kuttin, likes to say, when talking about Accountant relationships:

> *"It's not about the money. It's not about the money. It's not about the money. Until it's about the money!"*

There are multiple paths to monetizing the Accountant partnership (both for you and them). Which options are the most relevant to you will depend upon your business goals and compliance situation. We'll explore each path in this chapter, but it is critical that you (and your compliance officer) realize that there is no requirement to participate in any of the revenue sources covered below.

If you want to know more about the planning process, it is covered extensively in *"The Science of Running a Virtual Family Office"* (which looks at the VFO offered to Advisors' clients, but it is pretty much identical to Accountants).

In this book, we focus more on the different ways to Monetize the Accountant Partnership, and the revenue splits we'd suggest.

Advisor and Accountant Revenue Share Best Practices

There are many variables to consider when evaluating the *"fair"* revenue share arrangement between an Advisor and Accountant leveraging the VFO model. We'll review a few of the most common in this section.

Accountant and VFO Team Attend Client Meetings without Advisor

It is common for less experienced Advisors in our model to want to attend ALL client meetings with their Accountant partners. However, this can be very time consuming and draining on the Advisor over time.

For this reason, we would recommend the **Advisor ONLY attend client meetings when the VFO Services Team has identified that the client does, indeed, want a service within the Advisor's wheelhouse.** In this circumstance, the Advisor can act like the VFO Specialist within Financial Planning, Insurance, etc., allowing them to *"stay in their lane."*

Likewise, when the clients' needs are outside of the Advisor's wheelhouse, the VFO Services team will lead that client through the appropriate planning process and ultimately compensate the Advisor 10 percent from their share of any revenue generated (without requiring ANY of the Advisor's time).

Accountant and Advisor Attend Client Meetings Together

When the Accountant and Advisor are both attending meetings together, the overriding principle is that most of the revenue generated from the partnership should be based on a 50/50 arrangement net of direct costs (profit share).

The first five examples listed below are simple ways the Accountant can be compensated by the Advisor, most likely when revenue from the second list of examples below has not started to flow or cannot be shared due to the Accountant not being licensed.

- Pay Client Invoice from the Accountant in lieu of the Client paying it
- Pay Accountant Consultant Fee
- Pay Accountant's Miscellaneous Expenses
- Pay Accountant Event Costs
- Donate to Charity on the Accountant's behalf

More significant revenue sharing opportunities as the relationship develops. This remains in force as long as the relationship is in force.

- Share in VFO Specialist Revenue – 50/50 subject to significant direct costs being incurred by either party
- Share in Insurance Commission – 50/50 providing the Accountant holds the appropriate licenses
- Share in Security Fees – Range between 80/20 and 70/30 (Advisor/Accountant) depending on the involvement of the Accountant and due to the ongoing Client management by the Advisor. This assumes the Accountant holds the appropriate licenses or paid via Solicitor Agreement
- Tax Planning Fees or VFO Client Membership Fees – 50/50 if sharing in commissions and security fees. If not, then the Accountant could receive a larger percent of these fees to balance revenue (varies between partnerships)

VFO Fast Track Revenue Share

When VFO Services is responsible for leading the Accountants' clients through the Engage, Monetize, and Maintain phases, the following revenue share arrangement will apply.

- Advisor/Accountant keep **100 percent of the AUM or Financial Planning**
- Advisor/Accountant keep **100 percent of the Life Insurance or Annuities** *(unless VFO Specialist required)*
- Advisor/Accountant keep standard *"member share"* of **VFO Specialist Revenue**

- VFO Services and Advisor/Accountant split **VFO Client Membership Fees** 50/50 *(aka Proactive Planning Fees)*
- VFO Services and Advisor/Accountant split **Tax Planning Fees** 33/33/33 *(to pay VFO Advanced Tax Planner)*

PART 11

Maintain the Relationship

Like all good relationships, your Accountant partnership will require time, energy, and patience. We encourage you to evolve your mindset - Accountants are NOT a referral source. They're a valuable strategic partnership, and many partnerships will develop genuine friendships.

As the relationship matures and the Accountant becomes open to larger client announcements, we have a number of tools that can help. In the final chapter of this book, we will share details on how you can access these templates and pre-written campaigns, as well as others like them, for free.

- Accountant Announcement Letter to Clients
- Accountant Client Needs Review Form
- Accounting and Financial Needs Brochure
- Business Planning Brochure
- Retirement Planning Brochure

- Elite Marketing Services
- *"Introducing Financial Advisor Partnership"* Campaign

The *"Orange Tree Story"*

When discussing the *"Maintain"* step of the Accountant partnership, Anton likes to share a story that drives the point home.

> "When growing up in San Diego, California, my neighbors had a very large orange tree that produced more oranges than they ever could eat! As a result, they were happy to let us kids go in their backyard and pick oranges any time we wanted.
>
> For years, we would take them for snacks at soccer practices or make orange juice to sell on the neighborhood corner.
>
> At some point in middle school, the neighbors sold the house, and a younger man moved in. Unfortunately, he wasn't as happy about kids randomly jumping his fence and taking his oranges. He spoke to my parents, and our endless orange supply came to a screeching halt.
>
> To show his support, my dad (elementary school teacher and Eagle Scout), offered to take me to the local nursery and buy orange tree seeds. Brilliant idea - I didn't need someone else's tree - I'd grow my own!
>
> Unfortunately, after a week, all I had to show for my efforts was a little green twig coming out of the ground with no promise of producing oranges anytime soon. With that progress, I lost interest and left it to die."

My dad used the experience to teach me a meaningful lesson - **"consistency beats intensity."**

It doesn't matter how intensely you pursue your goals - if you're not consistent in your activity over an extended period of time, your efforts will never pay off!

Let's look at the growth of an orange tree as an example. Did you know that it can take an orange tree seed up to four years to produce its first orange? Some may wonder - why would you waste four years watering, fertilizing, and nurturing this silly little plant that's not producing any fruit? And it's a fair question, at least when you're only measuring short-term results.

However, when you shift your perspective and consider the medium and long-term results of that same orange tree, you see a very different picture.

A fully grown adult orange tree can produce up to 400 oranges per year, and live to be over one hundred years old! Think about that for a moment - the effort and sacrifice that someone made for a relatively short period of time can continue to produce fruit (results) for generations!

This same perspective can be applied to Advisors building partnerships with Accountants. We have had countless Advisors get *"fired up"* about the life changing opportunity that Accountant partnerships represent.

However, the majority will give up long before the orange tree really starts to produce. In fact, over 50 percent can't even commit to consistent activity for more than sixty days!

If you can commit to consistent activity, and want to shift from the lifestyle of a hunter (going out every day to bring home dinner) to that of a farmer (working today for next week and next year's harvest), then there is NO better way to do it than building and maintaining partnerships with Accountants.

One fruitful partnership with an Accountant can produce the equivalent of 400 oranges per year for your business.[9] Now multiply that times two, four, and six or more Accountant partnerships, and you start to see the true potential. And most importantly, if you maintain the partnership with care and intention - it can last a lifetime.

So what do you say . . . are you in? If so, let's talk about the next steps . . .

PART 12

Next Steps – Your Journey Starts Now

Congratulations on reaching the end of our book!

By this point, you have discovered the power of the **Virtual Family Office,** as well as how working with VFO Services can make **achieving your vision quicker and easier.**

We hope our message has:

- Increased your appetite to be a "proactive, forward-looking" Advisor
    - For the benefit of your advisor clients
- Opened your eyes as to **how you can also grow your Advisor business**

To repeat what we said in the *"Art of Collaboration,"* reaching the end of this book is not the end of your journey. Now, it's up to you to take the knowledge and insights you've gained and put them into action. It's time to step out of your comfort zone, embrace change, and start to build the advisor practice of your dreams.

We know that change can be daunting, especially when you are venturing into uncharted territory. That's why we keep reminding you that you are not alone on this path. We're here to support you every step of the way and so is the vibrant community of like-minded professionals as well as VFO Specialists that we have built at Elite Resource Team.

If you are ready to *"take a deeper dive,"* we invite you to visit elitert.com/science-of-building-accountant-partnerships to access a wealth of exclusive resources, from templates, tools, and technology, to coaching and training programs and live events. Above all, explore our Virtual Family Office Specialists, who can help you to *"look bigger"* and provide wider resources at a stroke.

As we have stressed throughout this book, the transformation journey is not always easy. There will be obstacles and setbacks along the way and moments when you question whether it's all worth it. But we can tell you from experience that the rewards from this path are beyond measure, both in terms of greater financial success, as well as the personal sense of fulfillment that comes from truly making a difference in your clients' lives.

Here's to your success and to the amazing things we know you will achieve.

Anton Anderson and Paul Latham

Frequently Asked Questions

Q1 - Explain the three types of Financial Advisor and how that impacts building partnerships with Accountants

As we explained in Part 2, very simplistically there are **three broad types of Financial Advisor**:

Those who have a vision to offer wider advice to their best clients (via the Virtual Family Office) – and are:

1. Not overly constrained by compliance factors
   - Can offer wider advice via VFO and can accept revenue share from VFO Specialists
2. Somewhat constrained by compliance factors.
   - Can offer wider advice via VFO but cannot accept revenue share from VFO Specialists
3. Very constrained by compliance factors:
   - **Cannot offer wider advice via VFO** regardless of revenue share arrangements

All three types of Financial Advisors typically want to build partnerships with Accountants but for **slightly different reasons or motivations**.

Type 3 - Very Constrained by Compliance Factors

This type is the easiest to understand their motivation to build partnerships. As outlined above, Type 3 Advisors cannot offer wider advice via the VFO, and nor can they accept any revenue shares.

Type 3 Advisors want to grow their core business, and that essentially means adding new clients who fit their particular *"swim lane."*

Forming a strong partnership with an Accountant is a great way to do this, as one of our colleagues Jon Kuttin (a Type 3 Advisor) likes to say, ***"it's like fishing with a big net."***

VFO Fast Track is perfect for Type 3 Advisors because it means that they can help benefit the Accountant (via the gift of VFO Fast Track and access to VFO Services team), but they don't personally have to have any involvement with the VFO. In return, the Accountant will introduce the advisor to clients requiring traditional financial planning while introducing clients needing other services to the VFO.

The **VFO Associate route is a total *"no-go"* for these types of Advisor,** as they are precluded from helping the Accountant to access the VFO.

Type 2 - Somewhat Constrained by Compliance Factors

This type is slightly more nuanced in terms of understanding their motivation to build partnerships. As outlined above, Type 2 Advisors can offer wider advice via the VFO but cannot accept revenue shares.

They will typically be closer in behavior to the Type 1 Advisors and are **particularly attracted to the *"fishing with a big net"* concept** (to help win more core business clients).

Again, using VFO Fast Track (rather than the Associate route) is much cleaner for them because of their compliance restrictions, whilst the **VFO allows their clients to benefit from wider advice and best advice** (outside the Advisor's *"swim lane")*.

This is exemplified by Dan Riso (Type 2 Advisor and Elite Member) who says:

"My goals fit into the 'two businesses under one roof' principle - I want to ***keep my core business boring and scalable*** (winning access to the right clients) *- but I also like having a* ***totally separate planning business which offers clean access to wider resources that support my more complex clients.*** *Having access to the VFO Services team means that I can hold the hands of my clients and be able to* ***orchestrate but not have to execute the solutions."***

Type 1 - Not Overly Constrained by Compliance Factors

As outlined above, Type 1 Advisors can both offer wider advice via the VFO, and can accept revenue shares.

The VFO Fast Track allows these Advisors to **build *"two businesses under one roof"*** (with or without building Accountant partnerships), but the ***"fishing with a big net"*** idea **allows them to benefit from both core business introductions and introductions via the VFO.**

Where the Type 1 Advisor has *"learned the rules like a pro"* and has sufficient resource to service, the Accountant has the choice of either VFO Fast Track or VFO Associate *(assuming they don't mind the drawbacks of Associate route as highlighted in FAQ#7).*

This is exemplified by Abraham Cecena (Type 1 Advisor and Elite Member) who says:

"I love the 'two businesses under one roof' principle. I have chosen to concentrate my personal efforts on my core business, but the VFO Services team, working alongside a new VFO focused planning employee I have added to my team, means that I am aiming to 10x my business very quickly."[10]

Q2 - Explain more about how *"two businesses under one roof"* works in practice for Accountants?

We introduced this topic in Part 1. It is always one of the first things we talk about at Elite to new Accountant and Advisor Members. In fact, we would be failing in our fiduciary duty if we didn't stress this fundamental point.

In the ***"Art of Proactivity,"*** Paul Latham talked about the concept in detail as it applied to Lathams Accountants. In fact, in Chapter 6 (page 131), when we fast-forwarded to the modern day we said the following:

> ***"Fundamentally, the 'Team Based Model' understands that 'proactive, future accountants' must SEPARATE those two businesses under one roof."***

We went on to say that the sentence above is **probably the single most important piece of information** (in that book), **for accountants to consider, understand, and implement.**

It is almost as important for Advisors to understand in their own business (see ***"The Science of Running a Virtual Family Office"***).

However, it almost goes without saying that Advisors who want to ***"Build an Accountant Partnership"*** have to be aware of this when putting themselves into the shoes of the Accountant.

The concept becomes obvious once the Accountant understands that they can **only add value by working in the future via planning** (of whatever type - but let's say tax planning as an easy example).

By definition, the Accountant cannot change anything in the past or add any value to what has already happened. The Accountant's tax compliance work is ***"looking backwards."*** It requires a focus on being **efficient rather than adding value** (basically *"do the job right, first time, on time, for the agreed price"*).

In the ***"Art of Collaboration,"*** Paul Latham described how Lathams Accountants took this to the extreme, even separating their tax department into two parts with **"Tax Past Team"** and **"Tax Future Team,"** where the employees either worked in one or the other but never both together.

Obviously Lathams worked hard at implementing this concept over several years, but most Accountants have neither the time nor inclination to do that. This is why VFO Fast Track makes it easy to achieve that separation of compliance and adding value (as shown below).

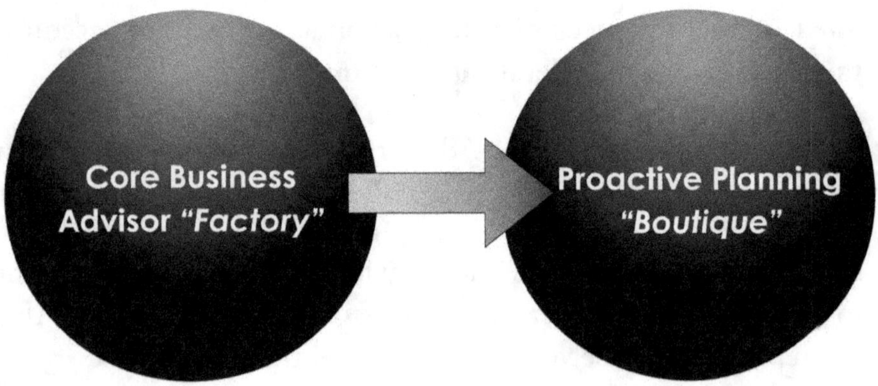

The Accountant retains their existing core compliance business as their ***"factory,"*** and purely focuses on **improving efficiency.**

VFO Services now and specifically **VFO Fast Track** allows the Accountant to simply ***"bolt-on"*** their **Proactive Planning "boutique"** with minimal effort required. Accountants only need to decide which of their best clients they want to **introduce to that extra added value.**

Crucially, this helps the Accountant to ***"LOOK DIFFERENT"*** to their competitors and will help them also win better clients in future.

By contrast, the VFO Associate route typically only works well **when the Advisor has a team and resources** sufficient to:

- Train the Accountant
- Attend every planning meeting with the Accountant
- **Create the second, "bolt-on boutique"** for the Accountant

Q3 - Tell me more about the Accountant's hidden worry (when partnering with an Advisor)? You called this *"Elephant #1."*

We explained in Part 2 that the Accountant will likely have some **unspoken fears** (about it being almost impossible for them to introduce all of their clients to any one Advisor).

Unless that fear is addressed, Accountants will get stuck with worrying about the clients they cannot introduce, rather than thinking about their fiduciary duty and the benefit they can bring to all their other clients.

The reality is that **no Accountant is likely to be able to introduce 100 percent of their clients to any particular Advisor**. VFO Services tackles that first *"elephant"* head on in the engage meetings and, in fact, **VFO Services existence is the answer to the Accountant's problem**.

Precisely **because** Accountants are also **working with VFO Services** via **VFO Fast Track for Accountants** (alongside the partnership with Advisor), the VFO Services Facilitator can reassure the Accountant and address their fears. The result is a *"win-win-win"* for all parties:

- **Clients Benefit:**
    - Access a model that **allows all their clients** to potentially receive **best advice**
- **Accountant Benefit**
    - Accountant receives the VFO Service at a **discounted rate** because of the **Advisor connection**

- Accountant generates new proactive revenue streams (see FAQ#5)
- Accountant has a **"second planning business."**

- **Advisor Benefit**
  - Advisor generates **new client leads for their traditional core business** (this is great for all Advisors, but particularly where the Advisor has compliance restrictions - Type 3 as identified in Part 2 of this book)
  - Advisor generates new revenue shares from VFO Services (where compliance allows)

By suggesting VFO Fast Track to help the Accountant (as well as themself), this will help the Advisor to begin to **build a trusted relationship** with the Accountant.

The **Advisor demonstrates from the start that they are looking at this from the long-term perspective of the Accountant** and not simply from their Advisor perspective.

Ultimately, as with building any strong relationship, it's all about "*doing the right thing*" - as well as **consistently maintaining a relationship built on strong foundations.** *"Consistency beats intensity,"* as you will remember from the *"story of the orange tree"* *i*n Part 11.

Q4 - Tell me more about the Advisor's hidden worry (when partnering with an Accountant)? You called this *"Elephant #2."*

This is simple. Elite have two types of Accountant / Advisor Partnerships.

- **VFO Associate Accountant**
  - Advisor trains Accountant in VFO process
  - Advisor facilitates the client discussions
- **VFO Fast Track Accountant**
  - VFO Services train Accountants
  - VFO Services facilitates their client discussions

VFO Associate Accountant Route

This is most appropriate where Elite have trained a very large and successful Advisor practice, and they have ***"learned the Team Based Model rules like a pro."***

That Advisor team has the **bandwidth and wider team resources**, as well as the **desire to service Accountants clients directly** and **without VFO Services involvement**.

That is great, but the reality is that those **Advisors must do all the *"heavy lifting."*** With the typical smaller Advisor firms (even where they have learned the rules and have desire), they are **limited to the number of Accountants with whom they can form a partnership**. Generally, unless they are a heavily resourced Advisor and team, that means only two or three Accountant Partnerships is practical.

The Advisor has to navigate *"Elephant in the Room 1"* in FAQ #3 above.

This route is clearly totally inappropriate for Advisor Compliance Type 3 (and maybe Type 2 also) as discussed in Part 2 of this book and in FAQ #1.

VFO Fast Track for Accountant Route

By contrast, this route is most appropriate where Advisor:

- Doesn't have time or desire to *"learn the rules like a pro"*
- Doesn't want to train Accountants in Team Based Model
- Doesn't want to facilitate every single client meeting
- Especially where the client is not interested in financial advice
- Doesn't want to do all the *"heavy lifting"*

Instead, the **Advisor does want** to:

- Enjoy the benefits of the Partnership for **traditional Advisor work flows**
  - Particularly for compliance reasons
- Enjoy the benefits of **VFO Revenues**
  - Where compliance allows
- Allow the Accountant to **escape "Elephant 1"**
  - Not make Accountant feel *"stuck"* to Advisor

- Enjoy the benefit of **limitless numbers of Accountant Partnerships**
    - Because they are not training / facilitating every meeting

It is safe to say that, since the introduction of VFO Services, **the vast majority of busy Advisors** (who are properly advised by a coach that truly understands what they are doing) – **chooses VFO Fast Track for Accountants Route.**

The majority of Advisors don't even entertain the idea of the VFO Associate Accountant Route – as bluntly, they have better things to do with their time. Most Advisors don't want to offer that option to any Accountants they meet via Partnership Fast Track.

Q5 - How did you arrive at an Average Revenue Per Client of $7,000?[11]

The average revenue per client of $7,000 was briefly referenced in Part 8 where we talked to the Accountant about them having a *"model problem."* See below for reference:

Better Math

What if average client revenue was $7,000?

100 A and B Clients
x **$7,000** Per Client

$700,000 Annual Revenue

So how do we get to $7,000 average? It's based on weighted averages and statistical probabilities.

The Accountant also actually has two potential approaches in terms of their preference regarding quality of life or business growth.

Approach 1 - Downsizing Business with Fewer / Better clients

We assume that 100 (20 percent) of the existing 500 above are already A and B clients, or they would not be a good candidate for VFO Fast Track (see target clients).

Those 100 are likely paying the Accountant more than the average compliance fee of $1000 already - let's just say $2000 each to be conservative - so the reality now is actually:

- 100 Clients x $2000 = $200,000
- 400 Clients = $300,000 ($500,000 - $200,000)
    - **Total Business Revenue $500,000**

If we said approach those 100 A and B clients, the probability (based on our experience) is that 60 percent will convert and generate a Holistic Planning Fee

- 100 x 60 percent x $4,600[12] = $276,000 x 50 percent (share) = **$138,000**
    - Based on the weighted average **Holistic Planning Fee**
- Assume 50 percent of those 60 will also choose to do Tax Planning
    - 30 x $22,000 = $660,000 x 1/3 = **$220,000 Tax Planning Revenues**
- Assume 18 of those (60 percent) will generate $17,000 VFO Revenues
    - = $255,000 x 50 percent share = **$153,000 VFO Revenues**

- That is a total from **VFO Fast Track of $511,000**
  - The original **Compliance Fees** were **$200,000**
    - **Revised Revenue Projected = $711,000**
      - **$7,110 per client**

Approach 2 - Retain the Compliance Business

Obviously the Accountant doesn't have to remove the other 400 clients who are generating $300,000 from compliance work (see above). See *"two businesses under one roof"* as described in FAQ #2).

Consequently, if you added that $300k as the Accountant *"factory,"* **total revenues would have doubled to more than $1m.**

In Summary

It is entirely the choice of the Accountant whether they want to focus on:

- **Quality of life - Approach 1** with fewer clients

- **Maximizing revenue growth - Approach 2** as illustrated

Final points: in reality, if the **Accountant was focused on Approach 1,** they should obviously build the revenues on the A and B clients first and then once they had done so, that would be the time to sell the other 400 C-D-E-F clients (PS - we have a VFO Specialist that we can introduce you to in that case!).

However, if the **Accountant was focused on Approach 2**, they need to make a decision as to **where they would personally prefer to focus**. Do they want to focus on:

- **"Compliance Factory"**
  - and leave the *"boutique"* to VFO Services and the Advisor

- **"Planning Boutique"**
  - and get someone else on their team to manage the *"compliance factory"*

Remember *"Monday to Friday syndrome,"* and don't try to manage both simultaneously, as it rarely results in maximizing performance in both areas.

Q6 - How are VFO Specialists vetted (why were they chosen and what is the due diligence process)?[13]

The process for introducing new VFO Specialists is similar across all five areas of the VFO (irrespective of whether tax focused). However, it is fair to say that we place extra emphasis on vetting tax strategies.

With regard to how a new **VFO Specialist is chosen initially,** they usually come from recommendations relating to a particular industry expert. Those may come from other Members or from other VFO Specialists or any other educational source that our VFO Liaison investigates.

With regard to the **due diligence process,** the illustration below is an extract from one of the slides that we go through with every tax planning client at VFO Services.

Tax Planning Details

VFO SPECIALIST ONBOARDING GUIDE

1. Initial Vetting & Credential Verification
2. Compliance & Risk Management
   Require third-party documentation evidencing strategy legitimacy:
   - Private Letter Ruling (PLR) from the IRS, or
   - Formal Tax Opinion Letter (TOL), or
   - Independent legal due-diligence report (e.g., Mick Law).
3. Technology & Data-Security Alignment
4. Process & SOP Alignment
5. Capacity & Scalability
6. Economics & Engagement Terms
7. Client Experience & Educational Resources
8. Formal Approval & Integration

Our due diligence process typically takes two months for any particular tax strategy to be approved and includes background checks, professional license verifications, and a complete documentation and research process.

As noted above, at VFO Services, when a tax strategy is being reviewed, we require either tax **opinion letters from tax attorneys** or **public letter rulings from the IRS.**

In addition, we have **due diligence attorneys on retainer to assist, and complete legal agreements to protect everyone involved.**

There are a lot of industry terms on the slide illustrated above, but in short, at VFO Services, we take the due diligence process behind VFO Specialists and particular tax strategies very seriously.

Q7 - Explain how the contractual situation works between all the parties involved (how does that impact revenue sharing and what the client pays for a particular service)?

This answer needs to be provided from a wide perspective to truly arrive at the appropriate context.

When the VFO Liaison brings on a new VFO Specialist, they do several things. They consider the Specialist from several perspectives (not only revenue sharing).

- **Due Diligence** perspective
  - See FAQ #6 above
- **Member Needs** perspective
  - Does the new Specialist fill a *"gap"* in the VFO Showroom?
- **VFO Specialist** perspective
  - Will the VFO Specialist benefit from being added to the VFO Showroom? Is it likely to be worthwhile for them?
- **Contractual** perspective
  - They need to agree to fit in with the tri-party contractual structure at ERT and VFO Services (see below)
- **Revenue Sharing** perspective
  - It needs to be a *"win-win-win"* for the three parties to the arrangement

In terms of the questions asked, let us particularly concentrate on the last two areas above.

Contractual Perspective

At Elite and VFO Services, we have a **tri-party contractual structure** that is **"mutually symbiotic."**

An example of a mutual symbiotic relationship is where, say, a clownfish gets protection from sea anemones while cleaning them, or bees pollinate flowers while gathering nectar.

We build a relationship where three parties win (four win, including client):

- The **Member** - and their **Client**
- The **VFO Specialist**
- **Elite Resource Team / VFO Services**

The contracts all link together to achieve this - and it works as follows:

1 ERT (including VFO Services) and Member contract

- Elite agree to provide access to three things
  - **Coaching and Communities**
  - **Tools and Technology**
  - **Access to VFO Showroom**
    - Includes option to do this via VFO Fast Track

However, we stress in the above contract, that when we provide access to the VFO Showroom, we are **making an INTRODUCTION** to the VFO Specialist and Member.

2 ERT (including VFO Services) and VFO Specialist contract

Essentially we repeat the above clarity in terms of what ERT are providing the VFO Specialist - where again Elite are **making an INTRODUCTION** to the VFO Specialist and Member.

It is very transparent and both parties understand totally - as well as the Revenue Sharing arrangements as detailed below.

3 Member's Client and VFO Specialist contract (engagement agreement)

Once the Client (of the Member) moves from MAP 4 to 5 or from TAX 4 to 5, then they are moving from **ADVICE** to **IMPLEMENTATION.** The client is in control, and they engage the VFO Specialist.

The level of the **implementation fee is agreed between the Client and the VFO Specialist**. Albeit the VFO Services team have a *"good handle"* on what might be regarded as *"normal rate for the job"* and can advise the client accordingly.

Similarly the VFO Specialist is aware of the fact that we know their *"normal rate."* They also know that if we are not happy with them, we are unlikely to introduce them to any future clients.

It is the definition of a mutually symbiotic relationship where everybody wins from the above tri-party contractual relationships.

Revenue Sharing Perspective

Part of the VFO Liaison's job in bringing on a new VFO Specialist is to agree the revenue share that Elite will receive (further to the Specialist contract with the client in Contract 3 above).

Each revenue share detail will vary in its amount because of different industry norms. The VFO Liaison will always try to seek a balance between what is *"fair and reasonable"* to provide a sustainable relationship. It's a combination of what is fair to:

- **VFO Specialist** - this is effectively a cost of doing business for them (like a marketing cost).
- **Elite / VFO Services** - we are doing all the *"leg work"* to make these arrangements and monitor everything that happens.
- **Member** - in terms of what they could achieve by themself.

Generally, and irrespective of the dollar amount paid by VFO Specialist to Elite (the gross revenue share), we will then in the first instance pay 50 percent of that gross to the Member as a revenue share (compliance permitting), leaving Elite with a net 50 percent share in the first instance.

However, if the Elite share (from a particular Member) over the course of a calendar year builds beyond targets and tiers, Elite will pay an ever increasing **Rebate** and **Membership Credit Notes** to that Member to reward success.

Advisor and Accountant Relationship

Normally, the Advisor and Accountant agree on a mutually beneficial revenue sharing and introduction basis between themselves (based on their individual circumstances).

There is no reason why the Advisor and Accountant relationship might not become firmer over time, and indeed in some cases we do see some Advisors and Accountants deciding to form contractual partnerships (usually with regard to work flows inside the planning "boutique," rather than their respective core businesses). However, that is not our presumption or how most relationships start.

In Summary

Ultimately, it is the strength of the tri-party contractual structure that really matters most. That strength is provided by the **"mutually symbiotic"** contracts between:

- **Elite and Member** (Advisors and Accountants)
- **Elite and VFO Specialist**
- **Member Client and VFO Specialist**

Q8 - Can the Accountant save money by becoming a VFO Associate, and put all their clients through VFO Fast Track via the Advisor Membership?

This is obviously theoretically possible, and the Accountant would appear to save $4,000 in VFO Fast Track Membership (after the discount).

There are really two ways to answer this question - the quick answer - or the detailed explanation.

Quick Answer

There is a saying, **"penny wise and pound (or dollar) foolish."** This idea is a great example of that term.

At Elite and VFO Services we like to talk about creating a *"win-win-win"* scenario (between Advisor - Accountant - Elite/VFO Services). Except for in unique situations, this idea actually creates a **"lose-lose-lose"** scenario, and for that reason, we don't encourage the Advisor and Accountant to go down this path.

Detailed Explanation

Let us go through **why in most situations the small membership saving "win" becomes an overall net "loss" for each party.** Once the downside is appropriately explained, we can explore the situations in which we would approve the request.

"Lose" for Advisor, Accountant, and VFO Services

There are four big losses that impact you as the Advisor, the Accountant, and VFO Services. Let's look at those one by one.

1 Training the Accountant

a. If the Accountant becomes VFO Fast Track, then VFO Services train the Accountant (and are paid to do so via the $4,000 Membership).

b. If the Accountant becomes VFO Associate, then **the Advisor trains the Accountant at their own cost and in their own time.**

c. The most important part of that training that the Advisor will have to do is with regard to **training the Accountant to invite clients to the Partners in Planning Meetings**. We already know that this is the single biggest area where training makes a difference to conversion rates. It is **highly doubtful that the Advisor will train the Accountant to the same standard as VFO Services.**

d. In addition, there is an added complication here, in that the **script will need to be amended** for the Accountant to explain why the Advisor needs to attend all meetings with the client and VFO Services team.

e. The result of the above problems will cascade into the Advisor and Accountant losses below.

2 Unfair Time Burden Attending Every Meeting for the Advisor

a. Notwithstanding the training time burden on the

Advisor to make sure the Accountant knows how to invite the clients to the Partners In Planning or VFO Tax Planning Meetings, there is a much bigger time burden, because the **Advisor will be obliged to attend in perpetuity every Partner in Planning Meeting** (as the VFO Fast Track is under the Advisor brand and irrespective of whether the Accountant also attends).

b. We discussed this in FAQ#3, and many Advisors will likely only want to attend PIP meetings with Accountant clients where there is a realistic expectation of the Advisor expertise being required by a particular client. Otherwise, the **Advisor is far better advised to leave the "heavy lifting" to the VFO Services** team (but that can only happen if the Accountant was VFO Fast Track in their own right).

c. Overall, this area will be a **huge, largely unseen, long-term time-drain for the Advisor.**

❸ Fewer Accountant Clients will Attend Partner-In-Planning Meetings

a. This will almost certainly be the direct consequence of the complications outlined in 1 above

- **Reduced client conversions** as described

b. However, also see FAQ#3 and Elephant#1 previously described

c. The Accountant will **almost certainly have various clients where it is wholly inappropriate to involve the Advisor.** A big benefit of VFO Fast Track is overcoming that problem. The clients get best advice, and the Accountant and VFO Services team handle the case (without the Advisor, who receives a commission from VFO Services even if they were absent).

d. The result here is that **some Accountant clients will be necessarily excluded and not receive the best advice.**

4 Lower Revenue Generated and More Time for the Advisor

a. The net result of all the problems outlined above is lower revenue and more time invested by the Advisor

- More training time initially
- Likely lower conversion rates
- More meeting time in perpetuity
- Fewer client meetings because of:
  - Likely poor conversion
  - Likely Elephant#1 (FAQ#3)
    - **Less VFO Revenue likely for Advisor**

From the **Advisor perspective,** the main benefit of VFO Fast Track for Accountants is the fact that the **Advisor gets to leverage the trusted reputation of the Accountant** and create a win for the Advisor.

Furthermore, because of the time factors as detailed above, by following the suggestion in the question, the **Advisor will be limited as to how many Accountants they can build a partnership with** (unless they are a very large and well resourced Advisory Firm).

From the Accountant perspective, the main benefit of VFO Fast Track is to **ENHANCE their reputation with their clients**. We explained in FAQ#2, how by **"bolting-on" their new planning business** (provided by VFO Services), the Accountant **"looks different"**

to their competition, and they will benefit from being more attractive to potential new clients, as well as providing valuable services to existing clients. Obviously, if, instead, the Accountant sends their clients to the Advisor for proactive planning, that is much more likely to **DIMINISH their reputation** rather than enhance it, particularly when they are sending tax planning clients to the Advisor.

Unique Exceptions

Now that we've covered in detail the numerous downsides of an Accountant choosing VFO Associate Accountant, with the intention of just sending their clients through the Advisors VFO Fast Track Membership, let's discuss the situation in which we would consider it.

If an Advisor has read all of the above points, discussed the downside with their Member Success Manager, and **STILL wants** to offer it to an Accountant, we will support them in that decision **AS LONG AS their meeting results stay consistent with other members of VFO Fast Track.** However, if their results, as explained above, suffer from this process, we will be forced to stop hosting new PIP meetings for clients coming from the Accountant's introductions, and instead strongly encourage the Accountant to go through proper training in the VFO Fast Track for Accountants.

In Summary

As stated, it is obviously theoretically possible to use the Advisor VFO Fast Track, rather than having an Accountant VFO Fast

Track, and the Accountant at first sight would appear to save $4,000 in VFO Fast Track Membership (after the discount).

However, this idea is typically ***"penny wise and pound** (or dollar) **foolish,"*** and creates a huge ***"lose-lose-lose"*** scenario for all participants.

This idea is the opposite of *"dipping your toe in the water,"* as some like to think, because once the **"genie is out of the bottle," it creates long-term problems that cannot be fixed easily by the Accountant.**

For this reason, VFO Services strongly discourages Accountants from doing this.

Q9 - Why do you suggest targeting Accountant Firms with one to three Partners (for building partnerships)?

This comes down to the **"law of probability."** Of course it is entirely possible to build accountant partnerships with larger firms, and indeed many Elite Advisors have successfully done that with larger Accountant Firms.

However, your chances of success are statistically higher with smaller firms in that one to three partner range. There are two big factors that influence this.

Factor 1 - Accounting Business Resources

As Paul Latham has said to literally hundreds of smaller accountants - *"you have a strength and a weakness. Your* **strength is your close personal relationship** *with clients, and your* **weakness is your relative lack of resources** *(compared to larger competitors)."*

You can say this to any smaller Accountant with almost 100 percent confidence that they will agree. Once they have agreed that they lack resources, the **door is wide open to the Advisor suggesting the VFO as a low cost answer to their problems.**

By contrast, the bigger the accounting firm, your confidence in making the above statement steadily reduces. In fact, with larger firms, **their relative size and resources is probably part of their existing value proposition to clients**. Whether it is true or not is immaterial. It is probably what they say and think. Consequently, the VFO is potentially seen as a threat and *"muscling into their territory."*

Furthermore, larger firms are much more likely to have several **existing relationships with other Financial Advisors** (across all the different partners), assuming that they don't already have their own wealth planning division.

Finally the larger firm will almost certainly have **existing resources when it comes to tax planning, and that is the most profitable area of the VFO by far**, so even if you persuade them that the VFO would be helpful in certain areas, there are almost certainly diminishing returns as the size of accounting firm increases.

Factor 2 - Agility in Making Decisions

This is just another fact of life. The **more partners** in the accounting firm, the greater the **"internal politics,"** and the **slower they will be in making decisions** (and the more likely that at least one of the partners will not like the idea).

In Summary

At Elite, we have been helping Advisors build successful partnerships with Accountants since 2014, and we have a pretty good idea what works best. Apply the *"law of probability,"* and you will be more likely to succeed.

Q10 - You mentioned three key attributes that the Accountant must bring. Which is the most important?

We said in Part 3 that Accountants must bring the following three attributes:

- Right **Clients**
- Right **Trusted Client Relationships**
- Right **Attitude to Change**

The answer to this question is very similar to when Elite Members ask Paul Latham which of the **"three ingredients of business success"** is the most important. The quick answer is that they are **ALL NECESSARY** by definition. However, in that case, **"desire"** is the key factor as you can get help with clarifying direction and **vision** and building a robust **plan**, but nobody except the business owner can drive the desire to implement the plan to reach the vision.

It is exactly the same answer here, as all three attributes above are **NECESSARY** by definition, because:

- It's pointless trying to build an Accountant partnership where the Accountant doesn't have the **"right clients"** *("mass-affluent," "high-net-worth," "successful business owners").*

- It's pointless trying to build an Accountant partnership where the Accountant doesn't have the **"right trusted client relationships"** (where the clients follow the advice of the accountant).

However, it's the third attribute which is the real differentiator, their **mindset and their attitude to change.**

Where the Accountant can see the **vision** to *"build two businesses under one roof,"* understand the **plan** to have a separate planning business, and bring the **strong desire to "look different"** to their competition, then you know that you are likely to build something special.

Endnotes

1 This refers to a specific historical transaction and is provided for biographical context only. It is not representative of typical outcomes.

2 Results referenced are based on internal program data and are not guaranteed. Individual outcomes will vary.

3 This figure represents membership as of the publication date and is subject to change.

4 Close rate figures are based on internal member data and represent a range of reported outcomes. Individual results will vary. These figures are not a guarantee of performance.

5 This represents a goal, not a guaranteed outcome. Individual results will vary based on market conditions, effort, and other factors.

6 For illustration purposes only. Figures are based on hypothetical assumptions. Actual results will vary.

7 Pricing and cost figures referenced are current as of the date of publication and are subject to change. Contact Elite Resource Team or VFO Services directly for current pricing.

8 Revenue sharing arrangements described in this chapter are examples only and are subject to applicable federal and state securities laws, FINRA regulations, and individual broker-dealer compliance requirements. Nothing in this chapter constitutes financial, legal, or compliance advice. Readers should consult their compliance officer and/or legal counsel before entering into any

compensation or revenue sharing arrangement.

9 This is a metaphorical illustration only and does not represent a guaranteed financial outcome.

Individual member experiences described in this book are not representative of typical results. Results will vary based on individual effort, experience, and market conditions.

10 Individual results vary and are not guaranteed.

11 The figures are hypothetical projections based on weighted averages and statistical assumptions. They are provided for illustrative purposes only and do not represent guaranteed or typical outcomes.

12 These figures are illustrative examples only and do not represent guaranteed or typical results. Actual revenue outcomes will vary significantly based on individual client mix, market conditions, practice structure, compliance requirements, and other factors. Past performance of other practitioners is not indicative of future results.

13 The due diligence process described reflects Elite Resource Team's internal standards as of publication. It does not constitute legal advice or guarantee the tax treatment of any strategy. Readers should consult independent tax and legal counsel before implementing any tax planning strategy.

www.ingramcontent.com/pod-product-compliance
Lightning Source LLC
LaVergne TN
LVHW022227200926
848481LV00006B/2153
* 9 7 9 8 9 5 0 5 8 3 1 2 4 *